*Twayne's United States Authors Series*

Sylvia E. Bowman, *Editor*

INDIANA UNIVERSITY

*Edward Eggleston*

# EDWARD EGGLESTON

## by WILLIAM RANDEL
### Florida State University

 45

Twayne Publishers, Inc.    ::    New York

TO
DAVID GRIFFITHS
WHO, IN OUR TIME, MADE THE TRANSIT

# Introduction

EDWARD EGGLESTON, if he could somehow review his own career, might regret the versatility that limited his achievement in any one endeavor. He would no doubt express general satisfaction with his continuing reputation as an American pioneer in both literary realism and social history. But he might be no less exasperated with the reading public now than he was in the 1880's and 1890's for remembering only *The Hoosier School-Master* while ignoring his later, better novels; and he would almost certainly wish he had lived a few more years—long enough to carry his projected *History of Life in the United States* beyond the two-volume fragment that he left. A man should not deliberately choose a multiple career unless he is assured of a longer than average life; Eggleston died three months short of his sixty-fifth birthday.

Realism and social history are both so important that we cannot be content with merely identifying Eggleston as a pioneer in each of them. Why does an individual strike out into unexplored territory, and what instinct directs him to mark a trail that successors eagerly follow and transform into a great highway? These two questions should not, perhaps, be linked. Most experiments with the untried lead to dead ends; only a few have significance for posterity. Simple human curiosity may explain the pioneering impulse, but the ability to anticipate great movements and profound change eludes easy explanation. If readers did not know that Eggleston deliberately set out to break the New England monopoly on fictional subjects and that he no less deliberately sought to infuse history with a fresh spirit, they might ascribe his contributions to sheer good luck— the lucky strike of the one prospector in a thousand whose exploration yields a rich vein of gold.

The pragmatic test, applied to biography, goes far beyond the label of convenience and superficial acquaintance. Readers wish to know not only the springs of action but also the individual capacities and limitations, the results of conscious effort, the formative conditions, and interrelationships with other men and with the total scheme of things. They wish to know the contemporary opinion, and the evolution of opinion and influence with passing time. Finally they are driven by a compulsion to fix upon an enduring estimate of value—what a man's life has meant, means now, and may mean for other men. There must be assurance that the individual is worth the effort that becoming acquainted with him requires.

The label of pioneer realist is the one most readily applied to Eggleston. Yet the chief prop to his fame as a realist, his very popular first novel *The Hoosier School-Master,* turns out, on objective inspection, to be realism diluted with elements better described as romantic and sentimental. Instead of reporting current commonplace actualities, it dips several decades into the past and introduces exciting episodes that suggest both the Gothic romances of 1800 and the dime-novel thrillers of Eggleston's own time. Characters tend to be stock figures or caricatures, not recognizable individuals; exaggeration of peculiarities is a violation of realistic integrity. Not even in the best of his later novels did Eggleston entirely free himself from these unrealistic habits, nor did he ever completely suppress the impulse to comment, moralistically or satirically, on the behavior of his created puppets. His best-drawn characters are mixtures of good and bad, strong and weak, but lesser characters fall readily into the extremes of black and white. Plotting and motivation are generally weak. The chief interest of his stories, admittedly, is the novelty of their settings—the local way of life in regions then unfamiliar to most readers. Yet with all these flaws, the term "pioneer realist" suits Eggleston better than any other term we might consider.

This term does not, however, apply to the whole of his published work. Eggleston viewed his novels as contributions to the history of American life, and his historical writing shows all the liveliness of fiction; but, even if parallels between his fiction and history were obvious to everybody, there remain other forms of writing that cannot be ignored. A large number of weekly articles and editorials might be excluded as mere journalism, but the omission would seriously weaken any examination of Eggleston's life in its entirety. Nor can his early juvenile writing be neglected—especially his Indian stories in *The Little Corporal,* or his voluminous Sunday-school writing from the period when he held a prominent place in religious education. Both the stories for children and the Sunday-school lessons had unmistakable influence on the didacticism of his fiction. Should he be classified as a clergyman-turned-novelist rather than a pioneer in realism? The type was not a rarity in nineteenth-century America. Conversely, in view of his firm final commitment to history, would it be best to call him a historian who found his calling only late in life? The novels, by this reasoning, would be considered apprentice exercises to his major work. Since he viewed his novels, quite early, as contributions to the history of the American people, this final suggestion is not wholly irresponsible.

Probing thus beneath the surface commonly casts doubts upon the validity of superficial classification. Moreover, it raises the question whether a man's life must necessarily be reduced to the limitation of any one identifying term. Men vary, of course, in the complexity of their interests; and Eggleston more than most men crowded into a relatively short life a number of careers —a few important, more of them brief in duration and trivial in importance. A reasonable alternative to the quest for a single, best label is to bracket him with certain other Americans, quite numerous in the late nineteenth century, whose restless versatility paralleled the post-Civil War chaos of shifting national direction: from rural to urban, from agricultural to industrial, from regional to continental.

The idols of the past were crumbling and new ones were still malleable, not yet firm. Uncertainty and abrupt changes in course were characteristics of the culture at large and of some men—such as Eggleston and James Russell Lowell, the older writer he most admired—with the native capacity for sudden fresh starts in unknown territories. They suffered, of course, by not staying with any of their interests long enough to achieve true greatness in one of them; but the variety of their lesser achievement and the results of their experimenting add much to their interest as American types. Eggleston was not versatile because the nature of his period rubbed off on him; from early boyhood he wavered between conflicting life purposes. It is more accurate to say that his versatility and his propensity to exchange one course for another found a market when versatile men were welcome. He was, in this (and in much more), very much a man of his age.

Yet it is primarily as a literary figure that Eggleston is remembered, and, more narrowly, as one of a small group that redirected the course of American writing after the Civil War. The cause-and-effect relationships between that war and the revolution in literature need not concern us here; it is enough to remember that reader interest after 1865 favored kinds of writing quite different from the prewar romanticism of Poe and Whitman, Emerson and Thoreau, Hawthorne and Melville. Mark Twain, William Dean Howells, and Eggleston were individualistic enough to run no risk of being mistaken for one another; yet they had more in common than any of them had with the venerated older generation. And it can now be readily agreed that all were realists, so labeled not when they first began to write but certainly by the 1890's. Many of the traits they had in common, moreover, have been shared also by subsequent writers, enough so to warrant the term "pioneers" for this trio. Despite his obvious aberrations from an ideal realism, Eggleston stands very close to what it is generally agreed that a realist is.

One hallmark of realists as a group is their limited formal education. College degrees were fairly numerous among the American romantics; the most successful realists, as a rule, have never attended college, or have left without completing the course. As one result, much of our realistic writing has lacked the polish of academic training, and some of it has been crude enough to suggest to supporters of the high esthetic tradition a falling off of literary excellence after the Civil War. The high esthetic tradition, however, was presumably incapable of the freshness, the spontaneity, and the strength that readers eagerly welcomed in the pioneering realism of the 1870's. Realism by definition treats of living actualities, not theories or refined artificialities; as Howells observed in *Criticism and Fiction,* no fabricated grasshopper—no matter how ingenious, how beautiful, how close to an idealized grasshopper of tradition —can ever match a real grasshopper. It is not alive. Colleges are not the best places to meet either live grasshoppers or other actualities of the sort that realists should deal with. They do not train men, either, in the vernacular of street and barn that Emerson had urged upon thinking men as an antidote to the crippling dependence on the past, the remote, the traditional. An institution far better equipped for the training of realists is journalism; and, by adopting journalism as his apprenticeship to realism, Eggleston was conforming to what has since become the established course of most of America's important writers.

Even more obviously characteristic of the pioneer realists were their birth and their passing of their formative years in the Middle West. The romantics they replaced in reader interest were all Easterners, representing the longest settled sections of the country. The Indiana of Eggleston's boyhood, like Twain's Missouri and Howells' Ohio, was well beyond the crudeness of its initial frontier stage; but for Eastern readers it was still new and different, and relatively uncivilized. Some feeling persists in Indiana that Eggleston confirmed the Eastern view of a retarded Hoosier culture by not explaining more clearly that he was describing an Indiana of the past—*The Circuit Rider,* for example, reaches as far back as the first decade of the nineteenth century. The better Eggleston succeeded in capturing the picturesque reality of his native region, the deeper and more lasting was this unfortunate impression of backwardness. However, the emergence of Eggleston's region as the first outside New England to boast a substantial literature is surely on the credit side, balancing if not outweighing any degree of wounded local pride. A truly retarded culture could not have produced an Edward Eggleston.

New England did not halt its literary output just because Eggleston was determined to break its monopoly. The shift of reader interest from East to Middle West was part of a newly awakened curiosity about the vast region beyond the Appalachians as an inevitable result, sooner or later, of the burgeoning national growth. Local-color short stories had already become popular, as writers exploited, whether romantically or realistically, the particular qualities of communities and sections. Eggleston's fiction, in full-length novel form, showed that the Middle West was not merely an outward fringe of population with behavioral eccentricities but a part of the country where people had taken root and could exhibit a continuity of institutions and a way of life no less real than life anywhere else.

The early realism had another advantage in what may be called "comparative sociography." Eastern writers, many of them, had gone to Europe and were equipped to compare the American character with that of older countries. The pioneer realists back-tracked to the East, where they wrote about the Middle West as it differed from their new homes—which were also the homes of most of their readers. Their frontier freshness, the novelty of their conception of American life, met an instantaneous response; they provided an entertaining and reliable means for the less traveled to become acquainted with different parts of their own expanding country. Henry James, continuing and intensifying the delineation of transatlantic differences, never won this reader interest; his art was superior to that of his contemporaries, but he chose the wrong subject matter. Eggleston might conceivably have stayed at the same crude level of art that is at once apparent in his first novel without losing his audience; readers simply demanded the subjects of his choosing. They liked his books for the reasons that attracted them to other realists—a vernacular flavor closer to earthiness than to libraries, a certain artlessness of style, and a tone of authenticity about a region that was rapidly becoming the most *American* part of the United States, as indeed it still is.

Eggleston's story is primarily the record of a search for expression, of a driving compulsion to make his mark as a man of letters. Few men have ever been quite so entangled in cross purposes, or so ready to abandon one course for another as he was. His fiction, closely studied, reveals much of this wavering in purpose; there are many allusions to his multiple previous careers. But he is not strictly an autobiographical author, for he depended no more, and perhaps less on his own experience than he did on what other men had put into books. The success of his fiction as a reliable representation of the life of his region depends on his sureness of touch as he interpreted his sources, and also on his remarkable accuracy in recalling local customs and localized dialect. Some contemporary reviewers thought he overworked these devices, and a modern reader, going through his novels in rapid order, may agree: soon enough, perhaps all too often, appears a chapter describing a corn-shucking or some other of the rustic customs that gave a social focus to frontier life. But nobody has ever seriously questioned the accuracy of his reporting.

As early as his third novel, *The Mystery of Metropolisville* (1873), Eggleston revealed a non-literary reason for writing his kind of fiction. In the preface he said, in utter frankness, "I have wished to make my stories of value as a contribution to the history of civilization in America." *The Scarlet Letter* and *Moby-Dick* also contribute to that history; many novels do, to one degree or another, if they have American settings and characters. *Tom Sawyer* and *Huckleberry Finn* certainly do, and so does *Main Street*. But it is hardly usual for an author to make such an assertion, and even less usual for him to make it so early. This extraordinary awareness of history, explicitly stated, removes any element of astonishment that Eggleston should turn, for the last third of his life, to an active career as a historian. He loved the distinguishing qualities of specific times and places that have contributed to the rich variety of American culture, and he feared for their survival.

In his preface to the 1892 Library Edition of *The Hoosier School-Master* he spoke, for example, of the distinctive Hoosier dialect "before the vandal school-master had reduced the vulgar tongue to the monotonous propriety of what we call good English." This attitude toward "correctness" makes Eggleston a pioneering member of the modern tribe of linguistic scholars who are under constant attack for tolerating "bad English." But more importantly, his expressed attitude toward local speech represents his preference, as a professional historian, for recording the commonplace actualities of early American history—the details of food and drink of the colonists, their clothing, their farm implements and household utensils, their medical practices, their superstitions—the very stuff, in short, of social history—with scant attention to battles and great names. In his fiction as in his history, accordingly, we find a consistency of viewpoint: a careful preoccupation with the ways of ordinary living of the American people.

The narrowly biographical, whatever its intrinsic interest, is admissible in a critical study only for its bearing on the kind of fiction and history that Eggleston wrote. It should provide the reason, for example, why he became a realist while his brother George, very close to him in age and sharing the same heredity and early environment, became a successful writer of ante-bellum Southern novels, which were sentimental, nostalgic, romantic. Chapter I reports, among other formative circumstances, an early fork in the road, with the brothers deliberately taking different routes.

As much as any other writer, Edward Eggleston was American to his very marrow, a creature of specific American circumstance, a product of the most American of regions, and a recorder of American actualities that he lovingly and consciously assembled in fiction and history. He was an individual, too—a particular American, hardly heroic yet a pioneer, serving his countrymen in a variety of ways but not always proud of the country he served. He was often too ill to be amiable; he was given, on occasion, to peculiar notions—some well in advance of the times, some out of fashion; he was driven by the typical American compulsion to produce and to succeed, and was never completely satisfied with either himself or his achievement. When, and only when, we as a people are fully satisfied with our achievement and are no longer impatient for a better future, may such men as Edward Eggleston become expendable.

A scholar soon learns to appreciate, and remembers with gratitude, the generous aid and cooperation of many individuals —librarians and others—in the accumulation of needed information. My greatest single debt is to the Eggleston heirs, represented by Mr. Elwyn Seelye and Mr. Edward Eggleston Seelye, who gave me unrestricted access to the Eggleston papers at Lake George, before their removal to Ithaca.

W. R.

*North Chailey, Sussex*
*August 1, 1962*

# Contents

# Chronology

1837   December 10, Edward Eggleston born in Vevay, Indiana, oldest child of Joseph Cary Eggleston, Virginia-born lawyer, and of Mary Jane Craig, daughter of a prominent local farmer.

1846   Father died, leaving Edward and three other children: George Cary, born 1839; Jane Lowry, 1842; Joseph William, 1844.

1849   Edward joined Methodist Church.

1850   Summer spent in Decatur Country; Edward's first exposure to illiterate back-country Hoosiers and their distinctive dialect. In fall, mother married the Reverend Williamson Terrell.

1851-  Family made its home first in New Albany and then in
1854   Madison, Indiana towns larger than Vevay, following Terrell's assignments as Methodist pastor.

1854-  Thirteen months with father's relatives in Amelia, Vir-
1855   ginia.

1855   Taught a few weeks in a Madison primary school; resigned because of ill health.

1856   First visit to Minnesota, May-August.

1856-  Methodist circuit rider, southeastern Indiana, Novem-
1857   ber-April.

1857-  Return to Minnesota. Methodist preacher at Traverse des
1858   Sioux and St. Peter. Married, March 18, 1858, to Lizzie Snyder of Baltimore. Daughter Lillie born, Dec. 15, 1858.

1859-  Various pastorates, alternating with business ventures.
1863   Allegra born, Nov. 19, 1860.

1864-  Pastor, Methodist Church of Winona, Minnesota. Blanche
1866   born, September, 1864. First Indian stories published in *The Little Corporal*, Chicago. Moved to Chicago in June, 1866.

1866   Edward William born May 29; died Nov. 4, 1869.

1866-  Associate editor and principal author, *The Little Corporal.*
1867   "Our Saturday Feuilleton," weekly column in Chicago *Evening Journal.* In demand as lecturer. First visits to Northeastern states.

1867-  Editor, *The Sunday School Teacher.* Western correspond-
1869   ent for *The Independent.*

1870   Moved to New York in May, as literary editor of *The Independent. Mr. Blake's Walking Stick. Book of Queer Stories and Stories Told on a Cellar Door.* Doctor of Divinity degree granted by Indiana University.

1871   Superintending editor of *The Independent* until August, when he became editor of *Hearth and Home. The Hoosier School-Master* serialized September 30-December 30, and issued as a book in December.

1872   *The End of the World.*

1873   *The Mystery of Metropolisville.*

1874   *The Circuit Rider.*

1875   *The Schoolmaster's Stories, for Boys and Girls.* Editor, *Christ in Literature* and *Christ in Art.*

1875-  Pastor of non-denominational Church of the Christian
1879   Endeavor, in Brooklyn.

1877   First trip to Europe, June-August. (Other European visits in 1880, 1885-1886, 1891.)

1878   *Roxy. Tecumseh and the Indian Prophet,* first of series *Famous American Indians,* co-authored with daughter Lillie Eggleston Seelye.

1879   *Pocahontas. Brant and Red Jacket.*

1880   In Europe until August, with family. *Montezuma and the Conquest of Mexico.* Turned to the writing of American history.

1882   Co-founder of Authors' Club.

1883   *The Hoosier School-Boy.* Co-founder of American Copyright League. Elected to Century Association.

1884   *Queer Stories for Boys and Girls.*

1888   *The Graysons. A History of the United States and Its People* (a text with several reissues slightly altered in title).

1889   *A First Book in American History with Special Reference to the Lives and Deeds of Great Americans.*

1890   Wife died January 27.

1891   *The Faith Doctor.* Married to Frances Goode, a second cousin once removed, on September 14.

1893   *Duffels,* collected short stories. Doctor of Humane Letters degree granted by Allegheny College.

1895   *Stories of American Life and Adventure. Stories of Great Americans for Little Americans.*

1896   *The Beginners of a Nation,* in series "A History of Life in the United States."

1900   "The New History," presidential address, American Historical Association.

1901   *The Transit of Civilization,* in series "A History of Life in the United States."

1902   Died at Lake George, September 4.

CHAPTER *1*

# The Making of a Realist

## I  *Indiana Boyhood*

"**B**UT THIS I MAY SAY, I had the good fortune to be born in a family in which literary acquirement was esteemed above everything else after religion."[1] So wrote Edward Eggleston in 1890, and there is little reason to doubt him. All four of the children of Joseph Cary Eggleston became authors— Edward, the most famous; George, hardly less successful; Jennie and young Joseph qualifying, though barely, with a single book apiece. Religion fared less well with the passing years: Jennie maintained her lifelong piety, but her three brothers strayed far from their early Methodism.

The books the four wrote, however, were so varied as to make us wonder how siblings with identical heredity and early environment could develop such different temperaments. Edward became a realist; George made his mark as a romantic of the Old South variety; Jennie published a temperance novel, *Gray Heads on Green Shoulders;* and Joe—poor Joe, whose life was an almost unbroken sequence of failures—never did find a publisher for his well-named novel, *Carry Me Back.*[2] The only difference in their environment is that the father, by dying young, in 1846, had varying lengths of time to be a direct shaping influence—almost nine years for Edward, only two years for Willie (as Joe was first called). Their mother, a woman of good family, sincerity equal to her husband's, and greater piety, but with much less formal education, exercised somewhat less influence. Left in straitened circumstances, she made the best of her widowhood, keeping the family together and trying, with modest success, to carry out her husband's plans for the children. She remarried in 1850 but died in 1857, an event that broke up the family. Jennie and Willie, fifteen and twelve, remained in the care of their stepfather, the Reverend Williamson Terrell;[3] but it is an odd fact that Terrell had his greatest influence not on these two but on Edward, in helping him get started in the Methodist ministry.

Despite his early death, however, the chief influence was the natural father. Joseph Cary Eggleston was born in 1812 in Amelia, Virginia, to a moderately prosperous plantation family. In 1829, soon after his seventeenth birthday, he graduated from William and Mary College with very high honors, though not the highest in the history of that college, as family legend maintained.[4] During the next year he studied law in Winchester, and two years later he moved to Vevay, Indiana. He was disaffected with slavery and wanted to live on free soil, but a more important reason for his move was that Southside Virginia was, by 1832, hardly a land of opportunity for an ambitious young lawyer.[5] The single-crop economy had worked well as long as the soil kept its fertility and newer parts of the South, with better growing conditions, were not yet offering competition; but the growing of cotton year after year had worn out the land, and even slave-labor was becoming unprofitable compared with Mississippi and other parts of the Deep South. Indiana, a territory in 1800, a state in 1816, had hardly begun to exploit its resources in 1832.

There is one further reason, perhaps the most important. Miles Cary Eggleston, Joseph's first cousin though considerably older than he, had gone to Indiana in 1815 and had become a judge of some eminence: one authority on legal history called him "the best-known trial Judge of early Indiana, if he has had a superior at any time in the state."[6] Apart from setting a precedent, Judge Eggleston, simply by his reputation, could help any other Eggleston who prepared for a career in the law. It was something short of pioneering, therefore, when Joseph Cary Eggleston moved to Indiana.

The people of Vevay, appraising the newcomer on his own merits, decided he was a prodigy and were not overly astonished when he met, wooed, and married Mary Jane Craig in a single day—May 2, 1836.[7] This at least is the legend; in a village of only twelve hundred people it seems strange that he would have missed meeting her in four years. Her father, the Reverend (or Captain) George Craig, a veteran of the War of 1812, was one of the local pioneers. He supposedly built the first block house on the Indiana side of the Ohio River, on a tract of two thousand acres of good bottomland; somewhat later he erected a solid stone dwelling.[8] The homestead, called "Big Orchard Farm," was about four miles out from the village. Captain Craig was in the Indiana senate, 1822-25; and he ran for Congress in 1833, the year he died.[9] It was a good family for a young lawyer to marry into.

But Joseph stood on his own two feet. He was a member of the Town Board, and probably its secretary, when, in 1836, Vevay was officially incorporated as a city[10]—a legal fiction for so small a place. For a number of years he gave the local Fourth of July oration, which no doubt helped him win a seat in the Indiana house of representatives, in 1837. Four years later, following the course of his dead father-in-law, he was elected to the state senate, for the term 1840-41; and in 1844 he ran for Congress, losing in a close count.[11] The summer of 1846 saw him stumping the county for science, lecturing on the new subject of geolgy; it was his last public service, for he died on October 21.[12]

Edward and George were born in the Vevay house that Joseph had bought when he married—Edward on December 10, 1837; George in November, 1839. Mary Jane had inherited a share in "Big Orchard Farm," and it seemed a good idea for the family to spend some of the time there each year, especially when Joseph's health began to fail. Jennie and Willie were born at the farm in 1842 and 1844, respectively.[13] It was a very attractive setting but, on low ground as it was, it could not have been the most healthful place for an ill man.[14] For Edward and the other children, the moving back and forth provided a welcome alternation of country and town living.

Writing for the *Forum* in 1890,[15] in the period of his greatest prestige, Eggleston disclaimed being self-made. When we consider how completely he was on his own from the age of seventeen onward, this disclaimer must be taken as a remarkable tribute to his father. Declining health had one advantage for Joseph Eggleston: it meant time at home each day to devote to his children, most of all to Edward, the oldest. Joseph's grasp of several languages gave authority to his advice to learn foreign languages, and Edward started early, dabbling in six or seven before he was twenty-five and never forgetting them. In 1897 he told an interviewer that he could read French,

Italian, Spanish, and usually Latin without a dictionary, German with one, and was taking up Dutch—all of them immediately useful to his writing of American history. His father also urged him to study mathematics. One rather eccentric notion of his father's was that a child should defer learning to write until he was ten; Edward learned secretly.[16] More concretely influential was the advice to buy every book he could, even if it meant going without a coveted bit of candy; in 1890 Eggleston somewhat ruefully admitted that book-buying had been his principal lifetime extravagance.

The farm was a lovely place, and Vevay was a very pleasant village. Eggleston always recalled it with a strong nostalgia—the unpaved sidewalks covered, in season, with crushed locust blossoms, the fruit trees everywhere, the flowers, the smell of the anvil hot in the smithy, the soft clatter of cowbells on the common. It all added up to "one of the loveliest villages on the Ohio River," as indeed it still is.[17] Culturally, however, it had the usual limitations of villages, and it was important what books a young lawyer might have in his home. The Eggleston private library, fortunately, had the reputation of being the best in town, a fact particularly important for Edward, whose early frailty kept him at home more often than in school. The books had been bought with no concession to immaturity except for a few that Mrs. Eggleston, pious woman that she was, thought should be available.

Thus Edward had quite a mixed intellectual fare—Jacob Abbott's Rollo books, Maria Edgeworth, and Todd's *Hints to Young Men* along with John L. Stephens' *Travels in Yucatan*, George Combe's *Elements of Phrenology*, and, among the last books his father ever bought, Hugh Miller's *Footprints of Creation* and *The Old Red Sandstone*. Edward read each book with the same seriousness; only later did he realize that books vary in reliability. But he took particular delight in certain ones, especially a two-volume *British Drama* and the collected plays, in the original French, of Racine, Corneille, and Molière. Lindley Murray's *The English Reader* introduced him to some of the best of English poetry.[18]

Staying home meant exposure to a different kind of education, surely, than attending the schools available in Vevay in the 1840's. When he did attend, the teachers found him a dull pupil until, at ten, he suddenly blossomed forth, becoming the pride of any teacher he had. The best of them was Mrs. Julia Dumont,[19] a writer of sorts who had the knack of encouraging pupils whatever their capacity. Eggleston always recalled her with gratitude. He remembered one afternoon being kept after school. He had written a composition full of phrenological ideas on "The Human Mind," and she marked it severely. But to his relief Mrs. Dumont explained that she saw in him the makings of a writer and a talent that deserved careful disciplining. He carried home her encyclopedia and read in it until midnight. On another occasion she lent him her copy of Locke's *On the Conduct of the Human Understanding* and guided him to Jeffry's review of Alison's *Nature and Principles of Taste*. Exhilarated by such heady subject matter, Edward sought for somebody in the village with whom to discuss the books; but he found nobody, and his momentary ardor soon cooled.

In all this early atmosphere of books, the one glaring deficiency, for a future writer, was in fiction. Contemporary Methodist opinion, which advised the shunning of novels as things not true, kept Edward from any acquaintance with the very kind of book that might have been most helpful later when he began to write fiction. If a novelist unblushingly asserted that the story told was true—a common device, especially among the prolific women authors of the period—the book might be admitted; this explains Eggleston's exposure to Maria Edgeworth and to all the didacticism that flowed from her pen. Her maxim "Waste not, want not" instilled in him a lifelong habit of petty economies that he later regretted. "Nothing is more to be dreaded," he remarked in 1887, "than a moralist or an economist devoid of all proportion."[20] Jacob Abbott's Rollo books had many of the same didactic qualities, but Eggleston recalled them with greater pleasure, especially for their suggestions of thoughtful observation of nature; and he was particularly fond of Abbott's "red-backed histories."

The variety of the books he read had a variety of results. The *Travels in Yucatan* prepared him for Xenephon, and thence for Vergil. The *Elements of Phrenology,* which he took quite seriously for a time, provided a lifelong topic for humorous allusion. Locke made him realize that the mind could be taxed—sometimes beyond its capacity. The Hugh Miller books, mildly pre-Darwinian, conditioned him to subsequent acceptance of evolution and of other scientific findings of the century. He later supposed that his emancipation from dogmatic theology took longer than for most people, and was more painful; the record shows, instead, that he moved faster and further than most people, reaching virtual agnosticism by the age of forty-two, with no more pain than most.

Two books that he remembered as having had a particular value in the development of his style are mentioned in one of the very few comments he ever made on the craft of writing. Since it summarizes his considered view of that craft, it deserves an extended quotation here:

> I do not remember when the dream of being an author began to take hold of my imagination. From ten years old I practiced writing diligently. I read Blair's Rhetoric, and Kamer on Criticism, but the good I got from these books was not in their rules, but in the habit of analyzing my own sentences, and of criticising my own style. It is generally forgotten by students of style, that clear thinking is back of all clear expression. To disentangle a subject and go straight at the kernel of the matter is the first lesson. . . . Felicitous expression, in so far as I am able to attain it at all, is the result of painstaking. As I grow older I work more and more patiently upon the details of expression, and interline my manuscript, to the sad discomfiture of printers. I have lost my early fluency in this strife after better expression, this endeavor to avoid the hackneyed, and to find truer and more varied arrangement of thought and language; for prose has its rhythm as well as poetry. I sometimes think good prose is harder of achievement than good poetry. After all, my ideal stands away ahead and mocks at my achievement. I come so far short of what I seek that it seems presumptuous for me to make suggestions upon the subject.[21]

What a man recalls late in life is not always an altogether trustworthy testament. Concerning his early reading Eggleston is no doubt as accurate as he is in his uncanny memory for dialect; his memory was somewhat less reliable (unless he deliberately suppressed the darker images) when he summoned up his remembrance of boyhood life. Vevay took on rather a golden haze, the way Portland was gilded over in Longfellow's "My Lost Youth"; it was simply better to recall the hours of happy play in the fine beech and maple woods near town, and the sober discussions with George about the actual speed of a train that was said to go a mile a minute, and the discarded type outside the printshop that he tried in vain to set in wood, and, a little later, when he had learned to set type, the compositions he composed for the *Reveille,* though they were never printed.[22] The bouts of illness seemed, in retrospect, a small price to pay for the hours of reading at home. But in all this he was indulging an elderly man's privilege of forgetting the utter wretchedness of much of his boyhood, as he began to record it in his journal in 1854.

Poor health was not the only cause for his recurring wretchedness. When Edward was three, in 1841, the Millerite notion that the world would soon end had reached its hysterical peak, as he reported it in his second novel, *The End of the World* (1872). It seems unlikely that he recalled any of its excitement personally, not because of his age but because a different religious excitement centered just then in the Vevay Methodist Church that was just across the street from the Eggleston home. Toward the end of a protracted revival, in 1841, his parents joined the church and had their two sons baptized. To this church, in 1843, came the Reverend Thomas Goodwin, who was impressed by the young lawyer's library but found it woefully lacking in religious books. Joseph handed him two fifty-dollar bills one day and bade him buy whatever he thought best on his next visit to Cincinnati. As a result, the family bookshelves soon contained such works as Adam Clarke's *Commentaries on the New Testament,* John Fletcher's *Appeal on Man's Corrupt and Lost Estate,* Richard Watson's *Theological Institutes* and *Life of John Wesley,* and Wesley's *Sermons.*[23]

It was no doubt the exposure to Wesley, reinforcing a book read earlier, *Todd's Hints to Young Men,* that led Edward into some of the most absurd behavior a lad of twelve or thirteen ever exhibited, for he set for himself a regime of the sort that Wesley recommended for preachers: rising at four, praying on his knees for a solid hour; other periods of prayer at specified times during the day; strict silence broken only for absolutely necessary statements; and a very sparse diet. Study was supposed to be aided by hunger; the brain worked most clearly, it was thought, when the body was anemic.[24] If Joseph had lived longer, he would no doubt have found a way to straighten Edward out; but his mother could not cope with such behavior and may have been secretly relieved when it led, inevitably, to physical collapse, which was something she could handle. The lad supposed the breakdown was proof of insufficient faith but he was too exhausted to continue his effort, and days spent in bed, under the loving attention of his mother, gradually brought a return to sanity.[25] A sturdier youngster—his brother George, for example—might have stood up better under such alarming self-discipline; but George was never so amenable to Wesley's influence. It is saddening to envision young Edward, congenitally frail and an easy prey for illness, making things even worse for himself by too conscientiously following up what he read.

"There is no other way of writing vividly and familiarly except by saturating one's self." So thought Eggleston in 1897.[26] He went on to explain that, whatever his lifelong devotion to books, he considered the periods of non-literary activity of no less value. It was surely gain for him, as a boy, to spend his summers working on farms. His father had advised it, partly, no doubt, from a realization that too great an absorption in books could lead to serious imbalance. Edward never did become much of a farmer, however. One of his employers, years after, had this to say: "Ed could learn to speak French without an effort, but he could not master the art of planting corn. Sometimes he put one grain and sometimes a dozen to the hill."[27] The experience was one kind of self-saturation with a subsequent result: he could write with a personal interest in *The Beginners of a Nation* about the colonists' methods of planting corn.

A longer and more important break from the usual came in 1850 when the entire family moved to Decatur County to live in the home of William Itti Long, an uncle of Edward's mother. She taught school at Milford and Clifty, and Edward clerked in the Clifty store owned by a cousin, Merit Welsh, who doubled as sheriff. Farm life had differed from village life, but this crude hinterland settlement differed much more sharply. The customers included the first real Hoosiers the boy had ever met, and conducting business with them across a store counter impressed their peculiarities of speech and behavior upon him indelibly—to his great advantage when he took up the writing of fiction. Most of the people were rough; some of them—he could not know which ones—must have been members of a gang responsible for a wave of local robberies. Solid, respectable citizens were scarce; one such, whom Edward greatly admired, was the local physician, Dr. Smalley. Three years later Edward read in a newspaper that "Dr. Henry B. Smalley, a member of the M. E. Church, a Son of Temperance and an Exemplary man, with a student Harrison and 20 others were arrested with a gang of robbers at Greensburg."[28] The shock of it made Edward physically ill; he took to his bed. But it was one more kind of "saturating one's self," though the dénouement was nothing he had sought.

During the visit to Decatur County, Edward briefly attended a singing school, the closest he ever came to musical training. In December, 1850, when his mother married the Reverend Williamson Terrell and took the family to New Albany, Edward and George enrolled in the "Collegiate Institute" there; but once again recurring illness, probably asthma, cut Edward's schooling short. The next move, in 1853, was to Madison, which had a population of eight thousand, and was the most important city in southern Indiana. Terrell became pastor of Wesley Chapel. Apart from the advantages of a larger, more sophisticated community than Edward had previously known, Madison offered the chance to meet a cousin, Guilford Dudley Eggleston, who became his ideal for the moment. Guilford was able to transmit to Edward his own great love for literature and to offer practical advice about reading. The life of the intellect, through Guilford's inspiration, came to seem the most laudable of all human pursuits. On a practical level, Guilford taught him the value of keeping a commonplace book; and it was probably his prodding that led Edward to compete for a prize —a volume of Bryant's poems—offered by the editor of the Madison *Courier*. The one condition was that the contestants be less than sixteen years old. Edward was fourteen. He won, with an essay on "The Beautiful"; in later life he looked back on this as "the greatest literary success" he had ever attained.[29]

"A little later," as he reminisced for a reporter in 1893, "I began an extended work on 'Materials for American Literature.' All American writers of the time were using borrowed European imagery, larks, and nightingales for their books. I for one believed there is material in our own land for a worthy literature; we do not need the larks and the nightingales. I thought when I began this first extended literary work that I had started something worth the while. But before the book was finished I felt a conviction that perhaps its authorship was a worldly ambition; and I burned the manuscript. Shortly afterward I entered the ministry."[30]

Had he completed that manuscript, and if he had somehow managed to get it into print, it might have been a manifesto for the realism he later did so much to establish. The act of burning it was typical of the "fits of religious ardor" in which, as it seemed to him in retrospect, his "literary pursuits seemed a sort of idolatry." Here was a dualism of significance: his "road not taken" might well have led to a Methodist bishopric or, somewhat more likely, to a career resembling that of Horace Bushnell, whom he later came to respect and admire. But though he chose the road of literature, he never quite abandoned the impulse that might easily have taken him the other way. "Two manner of men were in me," he wrote in 1890, "and for the greater part of my life there has been an enduring struggle between the lover of literary art and the religionist, the reformer, the philanthropist, the man with a mission. The duality survives even today."[31] The immediate context of this remark was the struggle for international copyright into which he had thrown himself with total commitment, even though it meant suspension of his history-writing for a long, wearisome time.

In 1854, when Terrell became a traveling agent for the American Bible Society, the family moved back to their old Vevay house. For Edward, this meant school again with Mrs. Dumont, and then with the Reverend Hiram Wason in an academy organized by the local Presbyterian church. To the earlier acquaintance with geology was now added an introduction to astronomy, for Wason used as textbooks a *Geography of the Heavens* and Elijah Burrett's *Celestial Atlas* (1833).[32] Despite the many interruptions of his education to date, Edward was now at an age (sixteen) and of a recognized mental development to think about college. His father, man of foresight that he was, had bought a scholarship at Indiana Asbury Institute, a Methodist college subsequently renamed Depauw University. As an enrolled Methodist and the stepson of a Methodist clergyman, it is unlikely that Edward would have had any trouble being admitted. But the uncertainty of his health was a greater consideration than the irregularity of his schooling; it must have seemed a poor risk to send one son who might soon be forced by illness to withdraw when another son, George, with much the same intellectual promise, had no such history of periodic breakdowns. The scholarship was accordingly held for George, but he made use of it only briefly.

Whether college would have helped or harmed Edward is hard to say. The absence of electives, general in colleges of the time, would probably have been a handicap to a youth who had already learned the art of independent study. Even so, Eggleston's comments on education, written in 1890, may sound like rationalizing: "Schools and colleges—I do not say universities—are primarily for those who cannot or will not study without them."[33] Had he taken up the scholarship and earned a degree, it might have strengthened his impulse toward a theologian's career. If, having earned a degree, he had still chosen literature, formal exposure to traditional literature might have kept him from becoming a pioneer realist. But this is both hypothesizing and anticipating; other facets of his self-saturation need attention before Eggleston can be viewed as a realist, or as any kind of writer.

## II  _Virginia Interlude_

In the fall of 1852 an old chum, William Shaw, wrote to Edward from Indiana Asbury, urging upon him the advantages of college. Leaving home, Shaw wrote, was the best thing that could have happened to him; Edward too should get out from under the "parental roof."[34] At just that time, and often during the next year and a half, Edward was actually living apart from his family, clerking in one store or another;[35] but the first real separation was when he visited his relatives in Virginia from mid-June, 1854, until August, 1855, a period of thirteen months.

The Eggleston migrants to Indiana, Miles and Joseph, amply justified their decision to move by earning substantial reputations. Whether these two were the ablest members of their generation, or whether the new region provided opportunities of a sort that any Eggleston might have seized upon successfully, must remain in the area of speculation. The Egglestons, migrants and stay-at-homes alike, had solid reasons for family pride, reaching back to the first American Eggleston, Richard— who had arrived from England in 1635—and attaining a peak in the person of Major Joseph Eggleston (1754-1811), second in command to Light Horse Harry Lee in the Revolution and subsequently a member of Congress from 1798 to 1799.[36] By the early 1800's the Egglestons were related by marriage to other old Virginia families, notably the Carys. Their principal holdings were in Amelia County, southwest of Richmond, on the coastal plain but close to the Piedmont—the area is generally known as Southside Virginia. Two of their houses survive today, though Egglestons no longer own them: "The Locusts" and "Egglestetton," both built about 1725, both of ample dimensions with irregularly spaced second-story dormers.

It is ironical that the tidewater South, the region most devoted to agriculture, has some of the poorest soil in the nation, although it exhibits a considerable range in quality from its fertile river bottoms to its sandy hill slopes. Without abundant sun and rain, and without slave labor, such families as the Egglestons could not have maintained their plantation well-being as long as they did. The price of cotton, their one staple crop, rose during the 1840's, reversing a downward trend[37] and making possible the generous gesture of offering a haven, after Joseph died, to his orphans in remote Indiana. There was the promise not only of a life of relative luxury but also of an education at William and Mary or at some other old Virginia college. A degree from a Midwestern college no doubt had some value, but in Virginia a college degree was the key to social prestige and, potentially, to the highly prized gentleman's career in politics.

Edward set out on June 13, 1854, and after a tedious trip by omnibus and rail was welcomed warmly at Amelia; he was obviously loved and wanted here no less than in Indiana.[38] But it was not home; and, despite everything that his aunts and uncles and cousins could do, he never did feel quite at ease in Virginia. No doubt the slaves had much to do with it; even at Amelia Academy, which he attended as a day scholar for part of the year, the boarding boys slept upstairs and the family slaves sent along to help them slept under the brick arches in the basement. He could hardly forget that his father had repudiated slavery when he moved to Indiana; a decision to remain in Virginia permanently, benefiting from the proceeds of slave labor, would have been a repudiation of his father's principles, and also of his own prior free-soil convictions. To a girl like his cousin Betty Cocke, with whom he corresponded later, growing up in a slave economy seemed entirely natural; to Edward, it was morally indefensible. After thirteen months he decided that the only correct course, for him, was to renounce it and leave, despite the loss it would mean of real and potential advantages. The Amelia relatives never quite grasped his reasons for going, and in various letters urged him to reconsider.

It is typical of Eggleston's journal that any fresh start, or any important soul-searching new direction, prompted detailed recording for at least the first few days. Hence we know, from his own words, more of these beginnings than of the latter stages of each experience. The journal he began the day before he left for Virginia continued long enough to include his solitary trip to the mountains, in August. Natural Bridge awed him, partly because it was a "vast arch reared by the hand of the Omnipresent," but also because such men as Washington and Jefferson had once stood where he was standing. The mineral springs, beloved by old Virginia families who had come to consider them as virtually their private domain and who resented the presence of lesser beings brought in by the railroad,[39] had no strong appeal for Edward. He disliked the hotels as buildings with no books, and preferred mountain paths, where he met cadaverous natives and one small boy, lugging a meal sack, who might have been another Henry Clay. He listened to sermons, observed eccentric behavior, and was shocked by what he called the "fashionable vice" at the hotels: mild flirtations, card playing by guests of all ages, and women bold enough to invade the billiard rooms.[40]

Back at Amelia, nothing seemed worth recording until December 10, his seventeenth birthday: "I made my maiden speech today before a temperance meeting." Being paraded twice in a procession, probably to attract a good crowd, made him feel "like a culprit going to execution." On the platform at last, one committee member introduced him, and another had to tell him to wait until after an opening prayer. "Finally however I got through much relieved." It was an inauspicious first step toward an eventual highly successful career as a lecturer.

The only overt mention of slaves in this fragmented journal is a report of a Negro wedding; he played a small part by joining other juvenile scribes in writing the invitations. He had more to say, though not much, about the boys his own age, whom he considered "hard." Tying a coffee pot to a dog's tail was an example of their idea of fun. Boys in groups often descend to the level of their most vicious ringleaders; and, in criticizing such behavior, Edward may have been deceiving himself into supposing it represented a certain fatal brutishness in the South. As a visitor and a stranger, especially as a boy who took religion seriously and spoke publicly on temperance, it is probable that he could not readily penetrate the teen-age circles, and that this rejection contributed to his sense of alienation from the South.

On February 4, 1855, he began a "Private Diary," recording the mental anguish resulting from a sharp recurrence of religiosity. "Pride is my great enemy," he confessed. "It is the alloy in every good feeling I have." He rebuked himself for feeling proud of his own prayers. But the chief source of humiliation was his inability to pierce the pleasure-seeking armor of his associates. "I wish I could be instrumental in the conversion of some of my schoolmates." He thought that he alone, in the entire school, was a professing Christian. But this was no virtue. On February 11 he wrote, "O that I were perfectly holy." By the 25th he reached a decision that it was his duty to preach, unworthy though he was and deficient in piety, purity of heart, charity, and patience. Reading a book called *Religion of the Bible* early in March made him despondent; the author was flatly of the opinion that ministers should achieve the apostolic standard, and he wondered how anyone as lethargic as he was could ever hope to reach it.

For two months the diary lay untouched. When he resumed it on May 6, Edward reproached himself bitterly: he had let worldly interests seduce him from prayer and proper zeal. But he also supposed that God in his mercy had sent this test: "Nothing else perhaps would have weaned my perverse heart but this scathing blow." He had nobody to sympathize with him, but he was grateful to God for restoring him to the joys he had forfeited by being remiss: "I believe this season of trial to be an important epoch—a turning point in my life." Other trials followed—a moment of anger that plunged him into momentary darkness; a Sunday spent with politicians. On June 2 he wrote, "How have I spent this week? What a solemn thought! The actions the words the *thoughts* of another week are irrevocably recorded against the day of Judgment."

Did Edward reject Virginia, and the obvious benefits his relatives were quite willing to provide for him if he would stay, primarily out of revulsion from the slavery that was the basis for those benefits? This would seem a reasonable conjecture were it not for the diary, which points instead to a steadily growing discontent with the religious climate of Amelia —it was a way of life lacking, it seemed to him in his sternly orthodox value system, a serious commitment to fundamental religious principles. But the very irregularity of his Virginia diary makes another thesis possible: an alternation of moods of the sort mentioned earlier. In his moments of contentment he did not turn in upon himself; his diary, after the section describing the trip to the mountains, became narrowly an outlet for his moments (or seizures) of extravagant piety.

Contentment there was, however, as he recalled the Virginia episode years later; the Virginia visit was not without some positive gain. One afternoon, when he was alone at Amelia Academy, he drew a copy of Irving's *Sketch Book* through a broken pane in a locked bookcase: in 1887 he could still associate this book with "the brightness of a Virginia sky and the resinous smell of old field pines. All my old impulses to a literary life were reawakened by the reading of Irving."[41]

Three years after this reminiscence, he expanded his recollections of Virginia. The old country-gentleman pattern had fascinated him, he wrote in the 1890 *Forum*, with its hospitality, its sharp social distinctions, its chivalrous and romantic sentiments, its narrow local prejudices, and its laxity in morals— all adding up to "a curious anachronism." The disregard of danger, and even of human life, where family and personal pride were concerned was a barbarism; even so, it was noble in its way. He proceeded to assert (after thirty-five years) that even the mild form of slavery he observed turned him henceforth into an abolitionist; but, unlike the fire-eating variety, he had always resented the abuse heaped upon the individual Southern people. "I very much doubt," he wrote, "whether history will not conclude that a more moderate style of speech on the part of the anti-slavery men would have much better served their purpose."[42]

Despite the diary, Virginia clearly did not mean unmitigated misery, or a vacuum of observations as guides for future behavior. The visit did, however, end in a decision: to turn back

to Indiana and to work toward the goal of becoming a clergyman. He was home again, in Madison, on August 11, 1855, and
he thanked God for it. The next year his brothers, George and
Joe, had their chance at plantation life; they fell in love with
it, and stayed South. George inherited one of the old Amelia
houses, studied law in Richmond, and fought for the Confederacy throughout the war, first in the cavalry, later in the
artillery, with Joe as his aide.[43] In the long run, the defeat of
the Confederacy made their decision the wrong one, since
it wrecked the plantation economy they had eagerly embraced.
Edward's contrary decision, barren as it seemed in 1855, brought
an initial exchange of graceful indolence for the hardest kind
of grubbing out of an existence; but Union victory ten years
later provided the means for forward progress unchecked by
the almost total social and economic collapse that betrayed
George and Joe and millions of other Southerners. Religiosity
was the principal force opposing Eggleston's literary impulse
and deferring its development; but in prompting return to the
Middle West it yielded a great, if delayed, advantage.

## III  *Minnesota Preview*

The Virginia relatives, in their extended campaign to attract
the Eggleston children, viewed Indiana as a rude new country
and as no place for orphans to stay. Their opinions were remarkably consistent: they were indignant when Edward, after
he had become well established in Minnesota, tried, with
ultimate success, to persuade his sister Jennie to leave Amelia
and join him. The untraveled, especially people who have
comfortably lived for generations in one locality, are likely to
lump all remote regions into the single category of uncivilized.
In 1856, however, Vevay and its neighboring Ohio River towns
had much more in common with Amelia County, from the point
of view of settled permanence, than either had with Minnesota.

Indiana became a state, the nineteenth, in 1816. Not until
two decades later did migration reach as far as Minnesota,
which acquired territorial status only in 1849 and became a
state, the thirty-second, as late as 1858, two years after Eggleston first went there. The larger part of its area—all of it that
lies west of the Mississippi—was not opened to white settlement
until after the Treaty of Traverse des Sioux, in 1851. It was

truly a new land, and it was a big one as well, roughly the size of Virginia and Indiana put together.

Why did young Eggleston decide to go to such a region, antipodal to the Virginia of his first venture from home? Other newly opened parts of the country offered comparable opportunity, without the hazard of extreme winter cold—Colorado, for example, or California. Minnesota was closer at hand than these two great meccas of contemporary migration, but what tipped the scales for Eggleston, as for many other people of uncertain health, was its deliberately fostered reputation for salubrity; the very air in Minnesota was said to be high in ozone content and thereby beneficial to consumptives, asthmatics, and hay fever victims. The more pessimistic such individuals were of recovery, the more likely they were to risk the desperate last-ditch journey.

Privately and officially, the early residents of Minnesota sought to create a favorable image, one that would attract settlers and thus build up the population. Numerous travel handbooks described towns and scenery and were eloquently enthusiastic about new parts of the country; typical of these was *Western Portraiture* (1852), which provided exact figures about distances, railroad and steamboat fares, comparative living costs, and business opportunities. Minnesota, as a rule coming last in the handbooks because it was so out of the way, often received the most superlative descriptions. Magazine articles offered their own share of alluring verbiage; "Sketches on the Upper Mississippi," for example, in *Harper's Magazine* for July, 1853, was a very welcome boost to Minnesota pride. In that same year William LeDuc was sent to New York to superintend the Minnesota exhibit at the Crystal Palace, and in 1855 the territorial legislature appropriated funds to maintain an immigration commissioner in New York. By then there were four daily and fourteen weekly newspapers in Minnesota, all of which printed extra copies for circulation in the East.[44] Eggleston might not have been able to cite his particular source of information; he may not even have been aware of being a victim of propaganda. But he had come to feel, in the spring of 1856, that going to Minnesota was his only alternative to dying.

Glad as he had been to leave the uncongenial life of Southside Virginia, Edward was at loose ends when he returned to

Indiana. For a while he tried peddling Bibles, thus contributing
to an all-out campaign by the American Bible Society to put a
Bible in every house in the nation.[45] He also tried teaching:
his exact words, recorded in his journal,[46] were "I tried to teach."
But he disliked it and resigned after a few weeks, giving ill
health as his reason. Speaking precisely, this experience dispels
the notion that he never was himself a "Hoosier school-master";
but his primary school classroom in Madison, in the fall of 1855,
was a far cry from the one-room school of his first novel, which
was drawn from his brother George's subsequent experience
at rural Riker's Ridge.

Ill health was more than a convenient excuse for escaping an
unpleasant occupation. Instead of getting better, his health
further declined during the winter—and so rapidly that his
mother shared his belief that death was not far ahead of him.
She agreed, finally, to send him to Minnesota, and accompanied
her eighteen-year-old son by river as far as St. Louis. From
there the trip up the Mississippi to St. Paul took ten days.
Edward discovered that he was not the only passenger on the
"Ben Bolt" so ill as to be pessimistic of survival. But with each
day of improving scenery—the grandeur of Lake Pepin separating Minnesota from Wisconsin, and riverbank towns each newer
than the last—he gradually forgot his symptoms in a growing
exhilaration. Although his passage was paid all the way, impatience for the feel of Minnesota beneath his feet made him
leave the steamship at Hastings.[47]

Seventeen years later, in composing the first chapter of *The
Mystery of Metropolisville*, he could easily recall his feelings:
"It marks an epoch in a man's life when he first catches sight
of a prairie landscape, especially if that landscape be one of
those great rolling ones to be seen nowhere so well as in Minnesota." The arrival in Virginia had roused no such enthusiasm,
so long remembered. The only fictional use of anything from
the Virginia year, indeed, was the transfer of an actual Flat
Creek in Amelia County to the Flat Creek School District of
*The Hoosier School-Master*. (The creek figured prominently
in the titles of foreign versions of the book: *Skolelaeren i Flat
Creek*, Danish; *Le Maître d'École du Flat-Creek*, French;
*Der Schulmeister von Flat-Creek*, German.) But it is only fair
to note that, of all his novels, *The Mystery of Metropolisville*
alone is autobiographical in this way. Minnesota, of all the

places Eggleston ever lived, was the most remote from normal expectation and hence the most vividly remembered in later years.

He plunged at once into what he recalled, in 1890, as "the tempestuous current of frontier life."[48] He stayed only briefly in Hastings and then, like his hero Albert Charlton in *Metropolisville*, he went by stagecoach southwest to Cannon City, where he found a variety of jobs—carrying chain for a surveying party, breaking the virgin soil with a triple yoke of oxen—work unlike anything he had ever tried before. Summer farming near Vevay and clerking in grocery stores were child's play in comparison. He was too exhausted at night to suffer insomnia, or to think about being asthmatic. In a very short time he grew hardened and strong.

Letters from home reflected an alien world: his mother reported the snobbish behavior of some Virginia visitors; George reported the intense heat at Greencastle, and bade Edward be on the lookout for a good job for him; Jennie reported Buchanan's nomination and a Methodist conference that adjourned, shockingly, only after midnight; and Terrell enjoined Edward to take care of his health—"let everything bend to that end."[49] E. D. Long sent from Madison his certificate of membership in the Methodist Church and his license to exhort, which he found only one occasion to use in Cannon City.[50] Long also asked Edward to enter a land claim for him; he was confident that Minnesota would become a great state.[51] Edward, equally confident, bought a piece of land near Hastings that still bears his name, Eggleston Station. Homesteading, land claims, real estate speculation, and all the other facets of life in so new and energetic a region fascinated him. And seventeen years later their interest was still fresh; they comprise a more absorbing part of *Metropolisville* than the mystery itself.

When Rice County was created in 1855, Cannon City was named the county seat; but Faribault, three miles away and much better located for growth, was able to wrest that honor away in an election the next year. The rivalry was intense, for the losing town stood a strong chance of early extinction.[52] Hence the vigorous campaign by just such men as Plausaby, the land shark in *Metropolisville*, to find buyers of choice corner lots, near the conjectural Baptist Church and the even more conjectural university. The book somewhat exaggerates reality as Eggleston had observed it at the age of eighteen; but his prediction proved accurate, for Cannon City soon became a veritable ghost town.

The one surviving letter that Edward wrote from Cannon City,[53] perhaps the only letter he found time to write, is very informative. He had just received a letter from his mother that had taken twenty days to reach him. He reported having learned the "Daguerran art" at Faribault, but he was not sanguine about making much money from it. Even so, and despite a cash balance of only sixteen dollars, he asked that no money be sent. With the bravado of youth he was sure he could earn his own way. He advised against sending George: "Tell George to 'hold his horses' till I come." Preacher friends had been urging him to enter the Methodist Conference, but "I have no horse and wouldn't if I could." He had met some Indians and was studying their character. At the moment he was wearing a pair of genuine Indian moccasins. "I must come home and spend the long winter nights telling Indian and rattlesnake 'yarns'." Finally, in a hurried postscript, he added the startling "Latest News" that he planned to leave at once for home, on foot, by way of Iowa, Nebraska, and Kansas. He supposed he might reach Indiana by October.

Thus ended his initiation to Minnesota. In 1893 he told a reporter that he had hoped to see the fighting in "Bloody Kansas" but had learned, along the way, that nobody was being allowed, just then, to cross into Kansas-Nebraska territory. Turning east instead, he kept on walking until he reached Galesburg, Illinois. With his remaining cash and two dollars borrowed from a total stranger, he bought a railroad ticket and rode the rest of the way. He had walked, he estimated, 365 miles[54]——no mean feat for a lad who, not long before, had viewed death as imminent. Three months in Minnesota had done far more for him than he had dared to hope.

## IV  *Circuit Rider*

The alternation of impulses, literary versus religious, was quiescent during the short Minnesota adventure, as it had been in the early weeks of his visit to Virginia. Edward used the license to exhort just once; he had no time to read. The excitement and feverish activity that engulfed him in Cannon

City provided no occasion for morbid soul-searching about his
destiny; during those busy weeks he was almost entirely a man
of action, not an introvert. Once he was home again, however,
the old familiar circumstances reabsorbed him. He set about
securing an appointment as a preacher, no doubt encouraged
by his pious mother and his clergyman stepfather. He had
not been particularly interested in the invitation to join the
Minnesota Conference, but now he applied to the local Methodist authorities, and was granted this certificate:

> Edward Eggleston is hereby authorized to exercise his gifts as
> a Local Preacher in the Methodist Episopal church, so long as
> his faith and practice accord with the doctrines and discipline
> of said church.
> Signed in behalf of the Quarterly conference of Wesley chapel
> Madison—Madison District S. E. Ind conference held Aug. 28th
> 1856
>
> THOMAS H. LYNCH
> P. E.[55]

Edward could have had few illusions about the life of a
preacher. Terrell worked hard and with total devotion to the
Methodist cause, but he had little to show for it except spir-
itually; the family (with both Eggleston and Terrell children)
barely maintained itself as an economic unit. William Shaw,
who had written lightheartedly as a college student, had become a minister who now wrote in a radically altered tone:
"surely bro. Edward we should be glad we have the privilege
of engaging in such a work."[56] To the dedicated, self-immola-
tion was a virtue, and suffering was proof of success; the
supreme evidence of sacrifice was dying for the cause and
being buried in an unmarked grave.

Edward's mother, in former years, had often beguiled her
four children with tales of pioneer heroics—not so much
about anything she had witnessed as about the facts and
legends she would have heard her father relate. She was convinced that the early circuit riders were the principal heroes
of the frontier, and she had an inexhaustible fund of thrilling
stories about adventures fully corroborated in the autobiogra-
phies published by some of the famous circuit riders. Whether,
in 1856, Edward hoped to experience any of the exciting adventures of his predecessors is rather to be doubted; but he knew

there would be hardships enough and many occasions for exultation in physical suffering. He was introduced to the work of the circuit in its waning years; it was only an accident of chronology that gave him a firsthand knowledge of its actualities as a major frontier phenomenon. The catalogue of trials that he included in Chapter XX of *The Circuit Rider* listed some that no longer existed when he joined the great tradition: "Perils of Indians, perils of floods, perils of alligators, perils of bad food, perils of cold beds, perils of robbers, perils of rowdies, perils of fevers, and the weariness of five thousand miles of horseback riding in a year, with five or six hundred preachings in the same time. . . ."

*The Circuit Rider,* of all his novels, is the most intimate and affectionate; it deeply and seriously reflects a remembered sense of dedication and of personal sharing. It is easy to suppose that this is his most autobiographical novel; in one way it is. But after sixteen years he forgot, or thought it best to disregard, the utter wretchedness and frequent morbidity that he recorded at the time, day by day, in his journal. The book glorifies the heroism of the circuit, the grandeur of its tradition —it reflects the legend as he learned it from his mother and as he liked to recall it later. The journal records pessimism and defeat, subjects better suited to the kind of realism written after naturalistic determinism entered American literature in the 1890's.

The license "to exercise his gifts as a Local Preacher" was only the first step; finding a place for this exercise took a little effort. He learned the stock phrases known to all applicants for jobs: "Sorry, no vacancies," and "Too late."[57] An occasional local sermon had to satisfy him until November when he was assigned to the Lawrenceburg Circuit as the ministerial assistant to the Reverend R. M. Barnes.[58] This was the dream fulfilled; he celebrated the occasion by jotting down "My History,"[59] a brief summary of his life to that point, with this conclusion:

Here I am thank God a preacher What awaits me I don't know my health poor All the schooling I ever got was only about 2½ years. All I received after ten years of age mostly in broken do[s]es only amounted to about 20 months. I thank God for this for my ill health prevented my becoming one of those book worms which look like they were all cut off the same piece. This fact has made me improve my time better at home

One notebook[60] lists, with date, place, text, and outline, the first six sermons that Eggleston ever preached, all in 1856:

1. Milton, Kentucky, April 3, Isaiah 26:3
2. Cannon City, Minnesota, July 13, Romans 8:9
3. Madison, Indiana, October 19, Matthew 20:6 (Wesley Chapel)
4. North Madison, Indiana, October 26, John 19:30
5. Fairmount, Indiana, October 26, Ephesians 5:4
6. Madison, Indiana, November 2, Hebrews 4:9

The outlines suggest a careful preparation, a thorough knowledge of the Bible and an unquestioning acceptance of it, a decided preference for the New Testament and for the Psalms in the Old, but virtually no familiarity with systematic theology. After the first six sermons he omitted the outlines. One friend from his circuit days recalled later that Eggleston relied increasingly on his meditations and used relatively few Bible incidents to illustrate his points.[61]

In *The Circuit Rider*, Eggleston estimated that the typical circuit rider gave five or six hundred sermons a year. He did not himself preach at this rate; during his five months on the circuit—from November 15, 1856, until April 12, 1857—he listed only seventy-eight sermons. With ten preaching stations,[62] each of which he was supposed to visit every two weeks, he learned the necessity of repeating sermons; but he had to be careful not to give the same one twice to any given congregation. The circuit in the rough hills of Dearborn County extended fifteen miles back from the Ohio River and had many creeks to ford; it was hardly a sinecure, especially in winter.

The Barneses came to love and respect him, although they found him untidy in appearance and in caring for his room in their house. His studiousness impressed them: he read every book he could find, but particularly history, travel, and biography. One habit astonished them until they grew accustomed to it: he would suddenly rise from his reading, his head in his hands, and rush out for a long ride or walk, or to make a ministerial visit, and then return an hour later refreshed and ready for the book again. Another habit that distressed them was his wearing cotton clothing, thin socks, and low shoes even on the coldest days;[63] he had gotten the idea from a book, much as, years before, he had adopted a killing time schedule from a book he had read. To the Barneses' great relief, a certain Mrs. Hargitt, wife of a local preacher, managed to talk him into more reasonable dress. He had been critical of her for dressing too well, but in the showdown he was no match for her.

This studiousness suggests that the literary impulse, though temporarily suppressed by the dominant religious impulse, was still alive; its gradual revival may have been one of his reasons for leaving the circuit. On March 17 he visited Cincinnati (his last visit, he feared, for years to come) and decided to resume his study of the classics. Other reasons are found in "My Journal as an Itinerant Preacher," which he began on February 24, 1857 (and which he dedicated to "My Dearest Sister Miss Jennie L. E.")[64] With more than seventy conversions and accessions to his credit, he was reasonably satisfied; and God seemed to be too, for Eggleston wrote that even when he was totally unprepared "God always supplied matter." Such experiences as the one at Logan, on March 22, gave him a supreme happiness:

> On Sunday I preached at Logan. After I had concluded the people raised a collection as a present for me much to my surprise. When I attempted to express my gratitude I was almost choked by my feelings. The people all wept. God bless them, and praised be his holy name for giving me such an hold upon the affections of the people.

But the robustness he had brought back from Minnesota was wearing off and at the very time his literary interests were reviving. The next lines in his journal bracket these two trends: "Monday and Tuesday sick. I have read more than usual this month." By the following Sunday he had made up his mind to return to Minnesota, and was in doubt only about how to make the trip. He hoped that physical decline would be paralleled by increasing spiritual strength.

> I want to be *filled* with the fulness of God. There is to me, as I grow weaker, an ineffable sweetness in the communion of the Spirit. O I want that all absorbing, all consuming zeal, that sweeping tide of mighty missionary impulse bearing me on to earnest effort. I want the baptism of fire——

It is probable that Eggleston did not know just what it was that he wanted, or what was wrong with him; and the confusion of elements makes it no easier for us to know. Minnesota meant the hope of renewed health; but suffering for the Kingdom of God had an attraction of its own. By the first of April he was approaching a climax: he feared he was losing his sanity. His tongue sometimes seemed to betray him, and he prayed to be able to bridle it—his "unruly member." The only specific external trouble seems to have been caused by his open condemnation of the liquor interests which made Lawrenceburg one of the nation's leading whiskey centers; he "let 'em have it about corn and whiskey," he recorded. "They took it with tears in their eyes." But one gentleman tried to secure his transfer to another post. His journal is seldom so helpful, however. The entry for April 9 contains a long passage about some particularly fiery inner ordeal, so bad that he felt he could not ask even his best friend to sympathize with him. Although his conscience kept telling him his course was right, he predicted that mere rereading of the entry, at any time in the future, would cause him intense pain. The next day he reproached himself for lack of humility; and he recalled having made the same self-reproach in Virginia.

On April 11, while attending a Quarterly Meeting at Logan, he submitted his resignation. The next day he preached on Acts 20:15, "The Kingdom of God shall see my face no more." When he had finished, about two hundred "professors of religion" crowded around him to say goodbye. Then he went home to Madison: "My eyes not yet dry, with good-bye to some of my best friends yet lingering upon my lips . . . I am ushered into another scene, in the midst of brothers and sisters, whom I've not seen for four months. Truly the sorrows of life are transient as its joys." But pleasure of the reunion was to be brief, for he was determined to go to Minnesota again as soon as possible. His final entry for the "Lawrenceburg section" of his journal, written on April 27, 1857, is a curious one, reflecting both his current religious intensity and his intellectual interest: "O that the great object of my life were to gain heaven to prepare myself for it. Reading Hitchcock's Religion of Geology."

He gave six more sermons, from April 26 to May 24; May 3 he preached twice. He read Elisha Kane's *Arctic Exploration,* Chapin's *Characters of the Bible,* and Theodore Parker. He submitted to some needed dental work: it was painful, he admitted, adding that he was sustained by grace. He resolved to pray not just three hours a day (an hour in the morning, at noon, and in the evening) but also for half an hour at ten and three and briefly at each other hour. He had made such resolves before. He may have hoped, subconsciously, that so much time spent in devotion would throttle the intellectual impulse that kept stubbornly reasserting itself; he could not pray and read at the same time.

His final Indiana sermon, on I Corinthians 4:20, was on May 24. Just a week later he preached the same sermon in Cannon City,[65] where many old friends welcomed him and where he felt very much at home.

## CHAPTER 2

# Decade of Decision

### I  *Return to Minnesota*

EGGLESTON'S first three ventures away from home had all ended negatively—by repudiation of the Virginia way of life, by a quixotic whim to see the excitement in Kansas, and by a breakdown in health. All three had begun with a sense of seeking the unknown and with an initial zestful curiosity that neutralized, at least for a while, the struggle between the "two manner of men" that competed for the mastery of his being. The fourth venture was not merely a repetition of the second, for it was unique in taking him, by his own deliberate choice, to a region he already knew, one in which his first brief visit had given him confidence. It was different, also, because he now had a profession: he had preached eighty-four sermons; he was a veteran.

Cannon City welcomed him back and supported his preaching. Until he could be admitted to the Methodist Conference, he served as a kind of free-lance clergyman; his old friends in the local Methodist Church, and the people of nearby settlements, did not stand on technicalities.[1] A group of Congregationalists urged him to serve as their pastor. When Terrell heard about it, he gravely advised sticking to Methodism: "Let Congregationalism furnish its own ministers." Terrell also advised him not to be too precipitate in buying a horse to take him on the small informal circuit of his own devising: "hold on a little, some of those generous hearted sinners will supply you with one yet."[2]

Barely two weeks after his return to Minnesota, the joy of being there was jolted by word that his mother had died on June 15, from over-exertion while preparing to send George and Joe to Virginia the week before.[3] "From that grief," he wrote six months later, "my heart shall never quite recover."[4] But the news did not alter the new rhythm of existence; he missed not a single Sunday's preaching from May 31 until July 26. Terrell sent him twenty dollars by Bishop Ames, an old friend; and he made Ames promise to look after Edward by assigning him, if possible, to a post that would not be too hard.[5]

Ames met Edward at the all-important Methodist Annual Conference, held in 1857 at Winona, July 30-August 2; and he rendered Eggleston a greater service than Terrell could have foreseen. Edward was still as indifferent about his appearance as he had been on the circuit in Indiana; unshaven and unshorn, he was poor-looking material for a preacher. He had also mislaid his credentials.[6] The bishop had to convince the skeptical delegates that Eggleston was a good risk. He was admitted as a probationer and assigned to the mission at St. Peter and Traverse des Sioux, located on the Minnesota River about forty miles due west of Cannon City and on the western fringe of white settlement.[7] It may not have been one of the easiest assignments, but it was a good place for a beginner to gain self-reliance.

George and Joe were by now settled with relatives in Virginia; George wrote on July 25 that he had been there only two days before "Uncle Chastain" offered to bear all his college and law school expenses.[8] Jennie was the object of a tug of war, for Terrell and Edward urged her to stay north and the Virginians tried to lure her south. George chided Edward for his advice to her and said it had hurt their relatives' feelings.[9] Terrell told Edward that "if she goes *it will be for life* and she will be identified with Southern peculiarities for all time to come."[10] The argument continued in correspondence for a good many months; the only one who didn't take it seriously was Jennie herself. But the visits she made to Virginia eased the tension. By October, 1858, George regained his former easy tone toward his "big brother," and could write a friendly comment on their differing views about Negro slaves:

> As to slavery, you will pardon me if I say I think it a good institution, or at least productive of more good than evil. I know you differ. Well you are too independent to deny me the privilege of forming and holding my own opinions. After eight-

een months residence in the south I am thoroughly convinced that negroes are unfit to be free. But we will not argue the point. We differ *honestly*.[11]

On January 5, 1858, Terrell wrote to chide Edward for not writing; but, considering his preaching schedule, it is a wonder that he ever found time for letters. He preached regularly on Sunday, and sometimes on weekdays, at both Traverse des Sioux and St. Peter, and once a month at each of four small stations—Fort Road, Rush River, Goose Lake, and Pettijohns', with occasional sermons at four other places. The Conference year happened to be a short one, from August 3 to the next April 15, but the list he kept shows a total of 107 sermons.[12] This number is just one more than the number of books he owned in Traverse, carefully listed in the same notebook in February, 1858.[13] He was too sick to preach for the first three Sundays in September and for the last two in January.

At Traverse there happened to be a teacher sent out from Dr. Muhlenberg's church in New York, a widow named Lizzie Snider, with some nursing experience;[14] she took charge of him in both these illnesses. She was several years his senior, and this, together with the nursing, makes it fairly probable that she became something of a mother substitute to the twenty-year-old Edward. In the "Journal for A. D. 1858" that he began on January 6, he recorded many conversations with "Aiggin" (Lizzie with altered letters), who provided a sympathy he had never known before—or so he said. This novel experience measurably tempered the religiosity of his journal language, unless we can attribute Eggleston's increasing composure to the mere process of maturing. He still chided himself for being too careless in conversation, and he prayed for humility. But there was a new note to his journal: "Rejoice this morning in God with a clear sky," and "O how I love this hard frontier work," and "The Lord blesses me much in my prayers with L——," and "Bless the Lord for such a friend."[15]

From the time of his September illness, his gratitude to Lizzie led quite naturally to the possibility of marriage. He asked Terrell for an opinion, and got a strong one: *You ought not to think of such a thing now.* The reasons—extreme youth, and health so precarious as to endanger wife and offspring.[16] Jennie, in a letter of sisterly bantering, hoped the engagement would not be protracted;[17] and Bettie Cocke asked "Golimpy" to send a daguerreotype of the girl.[18] Edward deferred action, but not for long.

In the second week of January, when part way across a frozen lake, he was caught in a snowstorm. "Trusting in Providence I carried my compass in hand until I struck the road." The sorry result of the incident was his second serious illness of the Traverse year, typhoid fever or something very close to it.[19] Lizzie tended him, but he grew worse. "On Friday evening Aiggin and myself, whilst praying together received a very strong evidence that the Lord accepted us as a living sacrifice upon his altar—nor has this assurance left us since, though we have been much tried." Love, as all men know, finds a way. Life was suddenly sweet and beautiful, prompting passages approaching poetry. "I remember," he reminisced, "when a boy in business (mercantile) how it used to refresh me to go to the woods and there study my Bible, my heart, nature & nature's God. And then in the South on Sabbath how did I love to recline beneath the moaning pines and there like old Thomas à Kempis commune with Christ. . . . And even earlier than this when a boy of nine I used to love to kneel by some old log and pray."[20]

Even illness could not dampen his spirits. On February 16 he was crippled with neuralgia but "Was much blessed in prayer with Aiggin." Four days later he wrote, "My enjoyments are *so much* increased by conversation with *ma chere,* bien-amie Aiggin. . . . Sometimes my mind is disturbed about the future— but hers never is." The upshot of all this is hardly a surprise: on Thursday night, March 18, "Bro Kerns joined me in matrimony with Lizzie Snider (the Aiggin of this Journal). Afterward at family prayer the Spirit of the Lord was poured out copiously upon us as if to sanctify a union which has been so remarkably providential."[21]

On March 31 he was sufficiently recovered to record at length the entire course of his courtship. The words "providence" and "providentially" occur often, evidencing a deep faith in God's loving care. When he learns what a happy marriage it was and how very much it affected Eggleston's life for the better, even a cynic might be willing to concede that their meeting *was* providential. Fifteen years later Eggleston made public confession of his love in dedicating *The Mystery of Metropolisville*:

"To one who knows with me a love-story, now more than fifteen years in length, and better a hundred-fold than any I shall ever be able to write, this book is inscribed, on an anniversary." When the love-story ended with her death early in 1890, he kept his grief to himself except for two stanzas in a book of family memorabilia:

> I turn but see thee not; before my eyes
> The image of a hillside mound appears,
> Where all of thee that passed not to the skies
> Was laid with bitter tears.
> And I whose thoughts go back to happier days,
> That fled with thee, would gladly now resign
> All that the world can give of fame or praise,
> For one sweet look of thine.

## II  *Progress in Methodism*

The Reverend William McKinley, who met Eggleston at Traverse des Sioux and remained his lifelong friend, never forgot his vivid first impression of him: geniality and personal magnetism combined with apparent rawness and immaturity. Eggleston's capacity for observation and description struck McKinley as phenomenal: "He could talk more and talk better than any man I ever knew." What McKinley could not have known was that young Eggleston was cruelly deluded about this very fluency; he reproached himself for "careless conversation" and even prayed for help in controlling his "unruly member."

Of that first appointment McKinley said that Eggleston "did well, as he always did; and one of the best things he did was to get married."[22] Lizzie was just the person to guide him, quietly and with instinctive good sense, toward self-confidence and away from his notion that an active tongue, backed by a quick intellect, was somehow shameful. It was, of course, an asset, contributing much to his rapid rise in Minnesota Methodism and to the success of all his later ventures in public speaking.

The 1858 state Methodist Conference, held in St. Paul late in April, kept Eggleston on trial and assigned him as agent of the American Bible Society.[23] Sadly he wrote the news to Lizzie: "Tears will come into my eyes when I think of being so much away from you."[24] Viewed with cold logic—which could not be expected of a recent bridegroom—this was a good assignment for anybody ambitious for clerical advancement; one Sunday and another he filled Methodist pulpits in Winona, St. Paul, St. Anthony, Orinoco, Preston, Chatfield, Anoka, Red Wing, Stillwater, Minneapolis, Rochester, and a number of lesser communities.[25] It was like riding a circuit of the entire state (for Minnesota attained statehood that year). It also resembled the circuit in exposing the agent to frequent perils. On the night of June 23 Eggleston, caught in a terrifying prairie storm, was unable to cross a swollen stream. Aided by the lightning and a line fence, he finally managed to grope his way across, hand over hand, to a house on the far side, where he spent the night worrying about the fate of his horse and his buggy.[26] Other ordeals were less frightening but equally difficult, especially the crowded quarters of wretched inns, the uncertainty of meals, the constant discouragement over collections—for the depression of 1857 was taking hold and money was scarce—and, above everything else, the misery of separation: "Pray for your Edward," he wrote in July. "I do feel as if I lacked part of *me* when I am away from you."[27] Now and then he could add a light touch: "As the French would say I am 'toujours le tien'—always thine. O sweet if I write much I get homesick."[28]

Remoteness from his own family had more than the one dimension of distance. The varying responses to Southern life reported by his sister and brothers differed from his own, which had finally narrowed down to rejection; but the process of selection was one he could remember sympathetically. It was his past, their present. Terrell, midway geographically, voiced an extreme position on slavery that Eggleston, with his months in Amelia and his knowledge of both sides, could never assume. But what made almost any news from afar seem unimportant was the actuality of marriage and the miracle of birth. When he resumed his journal on December 10, his twenty-first birthday, it was not with the customary self-reproach for having neglected it, but with the comment that he was "the happiest of men." Five days later, Lizzie gave birth to their first child, a girl. She was given her mother's name, Elizabeth, but was always known as Lillie.

Domestic felicity was a treasure to surrender with reluctance: the Bible agency work, tearing him away from home, grew steadily more irksome. Early in the fall he appealed to the New

York headquarters to release him; he also sought the advice of Terrell (who urged him to stay on)[29] and of a colleague named Chaffee (who urged him to locate a church).[30] The agency cooperated by letting him go; it could hardly have forced him to continue against his will. The summary Eggleston drafted for the annual report is overly dramatic, but it does give a fairly accurate account of the life of a Bible agent:

> In the ten months, while my health permitted me to labour, I travelled from two thousand five hundred to three thousand miles, by private conveyance, through every variety of weather. I have preached and spoken nearly, if not quite, two hundred times. The amount of labor performed and of hardship endured can scarely be conceived. I have spent half a night in an uninhabited prairie in the most frightful rain and thunder storm I have ever known. I have several times been in danger of freezing—have frozen portions of my body at times; yet so highly do I estimate the work, and so cheering was the result of our labours in some cases, that gladly would the agent continue to labour in this great field did health permit.[31]

Eggleston's final sermon as a Bible agent was given at Rochester on January 26, 1859. He was quite ill during February but was sufficiently recovered in March to replace the ailing pastor of the Market Street Church (or Station) in St. Paul.[32] The salary was to be forty dollars a month, but the 1859 state Conference, confirming the position for the next full year, changed the terms to $100 a quarter with his rent of $30 a month to be paid.[33] Even so, times were hard and his salary was often in arrears, though it was fully paid up by the end of the year.[34] He found it a "cold charge" but kept hoping to strike a spark. When he conducted the funeral of a little child he wrote, "I was much affected and trust the seed was not sown in vain." In his impatience for greater effectiveness he considered evangelizing in the streets, but he knew it would wear him out.[35]

Success in the ministry—especially the frontier Methodist ministry—was readily measured in numbers: conversions, baptisms, size of congregation and Sunday school, and, inversely, backslidings. The figures, published at the annual state Conference, had a bearing on the appointments for the following year. A lethargic congregation Sunday by Sunday was disheartening to any preacher, and it was doubly discouraging as Conference time neared because poor results, as exhibited in the statistics, were unlikely to impress the hierarchy that determined any preacher's progress.

Twice in the month of September, 1859, Eggleston recorded in his journal[36] an uneasy sense of being an inadequate evangelizer. Other men could turn a church service into a veritable orgy of repentance, with sinners crowding to the rail; but he never could. His journal provides the evidence of occasional conversions, but it also shows copious discontent with the rate of their occurrence. He prayed earnestly for more power over his listeners. But apparently he did not pause to examine his style of preaching: he continued his earliest circuit-rider practice of speaking more or less extemporaneously, reorganizing the meditations that were suggested in large part by his endless reading. He shared with the most illiterate of his colleagues a weakness in systematic theology, but he could not have forced himself to share the hell-fire ranting that made them successful exhorters despite their ignorance. The inadequacy of which he was conscious was on the crudest level of preacher's work—making the "emotional pitch." What he did not seem to realize, then, was that crudeness had obvious limits; but his kind of preaching, well based in intellect, had no upper limit at all.

As practice improved his pulpit technique, the gap between his religious and literary impulses narrowed. Once it had been an either—or matter, but with time and experience the use of examples and relationships that he found in books grew in effectiveness. The illiterate spell-binders, who lacked the first notion of applying "book-larnin" to their preaching, could be effective only among listeners as ignorant as themselves; no presiding elder would consider assigning them to educated congregations. Eggleston may have looked bad on the record during his early years in Minnesota; but he was a man who could be trusted, increasingly, with sophisticated churches. On the neophyte level, success might depend on rigorous suppression of his impulse toward literature; but on higher levels success would be increasingly handicapped by the suppression. Eggleston clearly did not recognize this fact; he merely followed his own bent with this result.

Growth in intellectual interest and attainment does, however, carry the risk of weakened faith or orthodoxy or both. In his rise through the ranks of Minnesota Methodism, Eggleston remained orthodox enough; but as early as 1859, when he was only twenty-one, his journal contains a few hints of his subsequent religious evolution. On October 4 he recorded a "solemn covenant" to devote himself "unsparingly to God's service," yet he also wrote this sentence: "I am a skeptic naturally and I never ask for an assurance of anything I pray for unless it be a spiritual blessing."[37] Fortunately for his peace of mind, he could still experience the mystic sense of receiving this assurance, which is an experience denied to true skeptics. With the new center to his life provided by wife and daughter, this spiritual assurance came more readily; their presence, or even the thought of them when he was away from home, distracted him from the anguished self-torture so evident in his earlier journals. In a word, he was a happy young man—happier, at least, than he had sometimes supposed he ever would be.

The one barrier to complete contentment was continuing poor health. A "cold charge" could be endured; there was always the hope of a better assignment at the next state Conference. Illness was another matter, for it struck him down at unexpected times and showed no abatement of its threat. Lizzie was unwell in January, 1859, and the following November it was their daughter Lillie's turn to be critically ill, a new cause for anxiety. "Lord Spare her if it is thy will," he wrote. "Thy will not mine be done. O how I dread the thought of losing her."[38] The mere fact of loved ones ill reduced his morbid preoccupation with his own frail health; but he was still fearful that a particular illness, instead of causing a brief suspension of his preaching, might make him give it up completely; and "It seems that I would rather die."[39]

It would probably not have occurred to him, then or at any other time, that recurring ill health was related to the emerging pattern of his life. When illness forced temporary retirement, it also provided leisure for secular experiments. During the Minnesota decade he tried a variety of activities, some trivial but others important; each of them added some weight to the balance on the opposite side from religion.

## III  *Breaking into Print*

The year 1860, if not a turning point for Eggleston, was at least a time of more interesting and varied activities both within the church and outside it. The state Methodists, convening at

St. Anthony in May, 1859, had accepted him as a full member (No. 62 in a list that began in 1821) and ordained him; at the next annual Conference, at Red Wing in August, 1860, he was elected and ordained an elder; and, as chairman of committees on Sunday Schools and periodical literature, he wrote and presented their reports.[40] Church newspapers and magazines were so important, he asserted, that the circulation of any periodical not officially sponsored should be discouraged as provocative of partisan feeling within the sect. A second report recommended establishment of a Methodist paper in one or both of the "Scandinavian dialects"—meaning Swedish and Norwegian. A third report, cheerful and confident, he wrote as secretary of the Minnesota Conference Missionary Society.

Quite a different kind of writing, for a general audience, was a series of letters in the *Daily Minnesotian*[41] reporting a trip he took with an eclipse expedition, in June, 1860. Simon Newcomb, later famous as one of the country's great mathematicians and astronomers, and William Ferrell, a meteorologist famous for Ferrell's Law describing opposite deflection of fluids north and south of the equator, represented the federal government; the naturalist Samuel Scudder represented Harvard's Museum of Comparative Zoology. In such company Eggleston felt like "a kind of fifth wheel"; but the scientists accepted him without reserve and he quickly felt at ease with them. None of the three, he was pleased to find, smoked, drank, or swore. On Sunday, June 17, they asked him to read an Episcopal service for the day. "I am no Episcopalian, but I confess the service, under such circumstances, was more than usually sublime." It was the ideal church of the Romantics—a lovely grove in the Sauk Valley, under a Gothic arch of blue sky, with a light prairie breeze serving as Aeolian harp, and, for choristers, thrush and lark, sparrow and plover.

Scudder opened Eggleston's eyes to the specific beauties of nature, naming the wayside trees and flowers; impaling insects, he bubbled over, like any naturalist in any new country, with a contagious enthusiasm. Mosquitoes and roads grew worse; wagons weighted with scientific instruments often mired down; even so, it was fine country—Eden awaiting settlers. Boarding a steamboat on the Red River, the party met George Northrup, the watchman, famous in a small way as the "Kit Carson of the Northwest." He was just Eggleston's age—twenty-three—and he shared his interest in literature; he had a personal library of about a hundred and fifty books, and always had two or three classics along for intensive study. The scientists urged Northrup to serve as their guide to Cumberland House, the remote place in Canada that they had chosen for viewing the solar eclipse, but he declined. Eggleston also had to turn back, reluctantly, at Upper Ft. Garry (now Winnipeg); he resumed his usual preaching on July 22.

What made the year 1860 most significant for Eggleston, however, was the accelerating of his impulse toward the secular life of the intellect. On March 6 he spoke on "Béranger, the Poet of the People," for the YMCA lecture series;[42] the lecture was printed in December in *The Ladies' Repository*,[43] a Methodist periodical published in Cincinnati. Béranger, who died in 1857, was momentarily popular for cheerful poems about bourgeois Parisian life and for his unconventional poetic form. Most of the poetry that Eggleston had read as a boy belonged in the mainstream of literary tradition; Béranger's appeal to him suggests an inclination toward the commonplace that was to be significantly bolstered when, in 1870, he read Taine's *Philosophy of Art in the Netherlands*.[44]

The Béranger article was his second publication in a magazine; the first, the year before, had been a poem, "Waiting for the Daybreak," also in *The Ladies' Repository*.[45] He may, therefore, have been attracted to Béranger as a fellow poet, but one who achieved a level of quality that his own efforts never reached. Eggleston actually published a good deal of poetry in his career, more, certainly, than any of his fellow pioneers in fictional realism. Some of it was topical, for political satire; some of it, for children; some of it served a good purpose in his fiction, especially *The Mystery of Metropolisville*. He also wrote poems for an audience of one, in letters to his wife. It would be absurd to take him seriously as a poet, but poetry must be included among the evidences of his versatility, in the forms of writing as in his patterns of living.

Not long after he gave the Béranger lecture, Eggleston set down in his journal a "Plan of Study."[46] Reminiscent of earlier schedules for self-discipline, it lacked the extravagant concessions to piety which, if followed literally, would have allowed very little time in a given day for useful activity. The new plan says nothing about prayers at fixed hours; it is almost entirely secular. He was clear-headed enough to realize, however, that he was outlining the impossible and would be forced to forego much of what he wanted to do. Even if his health held good, he could not learn everything.

## Plan of Study

Hitherto I have studied too aimlessly. I have wandered from one thing to another without thought or plan. I have reproached myself with this and have prayerfully tried to choose a branch of study for life, but I have not been able to choose any. I love mathematics intensely but I am not willing to give up my lingual pursuits. I love metaphysics but I love physics as well if not better. I love criticism and also poetry. So I have halted. My mental proclivities seem to be about equally balan[c]ed so that I am unable to concentrate. I think that we Americans are in too much of a hurry to decide, and so I think I will give the next decade to general studies if I should live so long & then or perhaps before I will decide as to the indications of Providence in regard to my life-work. Adam Clarke said a Methodist preacher "wants to know everything." I am sure I desire to know a little or rather all of everything.

After this preamble, he listed his present attainments. He knew all of the ordinary mathematics, as far as Legendre's first book carried the subject. In philosophy he admitted little knowledge: some of Locke's writing, plus summaries of metaphysics and a few articles on psychology. His Greek was very limited, but in Latin he had worked through four books of Caesar, half a dozen of Cicero's orations, one book of the *Aeneid*, and Vergil's *Eclogues*. French he could read almost as easily as English and write with a fair degree of correctness; he spoke it poorly, however, and understood it even less. Spanish he had only just begun to study. In science, he felt reasonably familiar with geology, less so with astronomy, not at all with chemistry and physiology. He had smatterings of logic and rhetoric.

Not surprisingly, he was able to record an extensive knowledge of literature and history: Addison, Steele, Johnson, Macaulay, Jeffry, Lamb, Wilson, Rogers, Milton, Pope, Shakespeare, Dryden, Gray, Beattie, Coleridge, Young, Alexander Smith, Tennyson, Campbell, Montgomery, Hemans. Criticism he considered "a cheap way of lear[n]ing the character of authors with whom one is not acquainted from reading." He knew the standard American authors, but after naming Irving, Bryant, and Longfellow he added "etc.," leaving us in the dark about the others, although elsewhere he expressed his admiration for Emerson and Theodore Parker. His reading in history shows curious limitations: he had read Rollin in part, Prescott's *Mexico*, "some" Hume and Macaulay, and "some" United States and French history. "I hardly know," he admitted, "how or where I gained a general knowledge of history. I have read a great deal of stray literature that can never be counted." Then he added a direct appeal for understanding: "If this should ever fall into the hands of another I beg it will be remembered that it was intended only for my own eyes."

The final step was to sketch an outline of study for the next ten years. "I am satisfied that with my health I will never be able to accomplish it but I mean here-after to have a plan. . . . Of course I do not expect to carry out this plan in detail. I have made it for ten years for the sake of unity." The journal breaks off at this point. A friend suggested an alternative course of action—enrollment at the new Methodist college in St. Paul (now Hamline University) as a non-resident student. It would have been possible to earn a bachelor's degree without mathematics. But although Eggleston considered the notion, he seemed reluctant to surrender his habit of independent study.

At the annual Conference he had been assigned to Stillwater, an active lumbering town on the picturesque St. Croix River, just where it widens to form Lake St. Croix. It was in the part of Minnesota that had been settled before the Treaty of Traverse des Sioux; while not really old, less than three decades, it lacked the rawness of Cannon City, of St. Peter, and of the other brand new communities he had lived in and visited west of the Mississippi. His first visit to the Stillwater region in his Bible agent days had yielded an experience comparable to his discovery of Irving in Virginia. Waking early one summer morning, he had read Milton's "L'Allegro" beside a window embowered with dewy honeysuckle; looking out, he had watched lumberjacks riding a great raft of logs down the river. The memory of the experience was still fresh in 1887 when he wrote one of his reminiscences;[47] in 1860 it was so compelling that when his second daughter was born on November 19, he named her Allegra.

Life was good just then, better than at almost any other period; and he was grateful. "I will here record my system as it is at present," he wrote late in September.

I rise at six Read in the Old Testament in French six chapters four in the new in English. I have already read the New Test in French & when the old is completed it will be the completion of all the Bible. After the Bible reading I study one hour on my sermons and then write an hour on whatever article I have on hand. I then read Latin an hour, & Spanish a few minutes I read some English work at odd hours during the afternoon I visit in the afternoon & read aloud in the evening.[48]

It almost sounds as though church work were nonexistent. The afternoon visiting meant pastoral calls; he also sometimes went to the state penitentiary, Stillwater's largest institution then and since, to talk with prisoners. He did not slight his sermons, giving them on the average an hour each day—as much time as he spent on articles. There were also conferences with men of his congregation about a proposal to enlarge the church edifice. But the golden, memorable hours were those of relaxation in the evening, after Jennie arrived for a long visit; her eagerness to learn complemented his own. First she might read her French lesson with her brother's help, and then his turn would come: "Read aloud from Emerson's Rep Men."[49]

## IV  *The War Years*

Joe, writing from Baltimore in December, 1860, described Maryland as wavering on the brink of secession and characterized the whole southern threat to national unity as "this worse than madness."[50] When the madness led to open war, however, he dutifully joined George in the Confederate Army. Edward was no less loyal to the Union, although no duty was possible; it was a source of deep chagrin that he was considered physically unsuited for even a regimental chaplaincy.[51]

At the close of his Stillwater assignment in 1861 he petitioned the Conference for a superannuated status, and it was granted. The war was proving beneficial to business, bringing to an end the depression of 1857, and he may have hoped to share in the reviving prosperity. Two projects interested Edward: making soap and selling real estate. As a boy he had watched his

Grandfather Craig making soap on the old farm near Vevay; he would not have forgotten the process. During the fall of 1861 he busied himself buying ammonia (a carboy) and kaolin (a cask) from New York, and a large kettle from Chicago.[52] He set up shop at "the Soap and Candle Factory next door to the Swede church"[53] in St. Peter. He tried to sell his soap by mail solicitation but with indifferent success; his best results were from local sales in St. Peter and also in neighboring Mankato. His other project, dabbling in real estate, is more obscure. In May, 1861, he was offered more land[54] near the quarter section he had bought in 1856—the Eggleston Station near Hastings. But whether he bought that additional land or any other, whatever business he developed in real estate was not enough for him to write about or to keep him busy.

By early 1862 he became an agent for a subscription book, *Sketches of the Rise, Progress, and Decline of Secession.* The author, "Parson Brownlow," was a notorious East Tennessee opponent of the Confederacy. Sales were brisk; but, as had been true in the Bible agency days, the work meant frequent absences from home. In May, when the pastor of St. Paul's Jackson Street Church went off to the war as a chaplain, Eggleston welcomed the invitation to take over that pulpit for the rest of the Conference year.[55] The Conference, meeting in October, reappointed him; and he stayed in this pastorate, his fifth in Minnesota, until his health failed again in the summer of 1863.[56]

Minnesota's participation in the Civil War was somewhat limited by the closer alarm in 1862 of the Great Sioux Outbreak. Eager as ever for action, Eggleston tried to join the state troops hastily recruited to suppress the disgruntled, rampaging Sioux; and again he was rejected.[57] The only role he had to play was the dismal one of burying, from his church, twelve men killed within a period of two weeks by the Sioux; on November 4 he and an assistant conducted a collective funeral for seven of the victims. Eggleston had come to know much about the Minnesota Indians, both Chippewa and Sioux, on his border wanderings; but in 1864, when he began a series of stories about them for a children's magazine, he never let his young readers forget that the plains Indians were generally savage and dangerous; he was incapable of subscribing to the notion of the Noble Savage.[58]

His two contributions to *The Ladies' Repository*, his letters about the eclipse expedition in the St. Paul *Minnesotian,* and a lengthy excerpt from a sermon on "Christian Patriotism" in the *Stillwater Messenger* in May, 1861, were the sum of Eggleston's literary achievement prior to 1864. That January he had the satisfaction of seeing in print, again in *The Ladies' Repository,* a carefully written article on "The Bible in Modern Languages."[59] In part it reflected his deliberate reading of the Bible in French and other languages; it was also related to a "Scandinavian Paper" he prepared for the Methodist Conference and was his own share in carrying out his recommendation that the Conference establish a Methodist paper in Swedish, Norwegian, and Danish.[60]

On February 11, 1863, Eggleston began a letter but broke it off and filled the rest of the sheet with a "List of Hoosierisms"—about forty-five words and phrases that he recalled from his visit to Decatur County a dozen years before and no doubt heard occasionally from Hoosier visitors to Minnesota. Lowell's second series of *Biglow Papers,* appearing from time to time in the *Atlantic Monthly,* may have reawakened Eggleston's old interest in dialect.

Eighteen months later, in August, 1864, the latent interest found its first occasion for a practical outlet in a "Letter to General Gorman from a Hoosier" in a St. Paul paper.[61] Adopting the classical device of the earlier Western humorists, he created a loquacious, ungrammatical personage, Zoroaster Higgins, as his mouthpiece for a veiled attack on Gorman, a Democrat spokesman who had recently given a McClellan speech in St. Paul's Ingersoll Hall. When Eggleston became a pioneer in dialect realism, in 1870, he restricted the dialect to the dialogue, as Mark Twain was to do in *Tom Sawyer;* but this first experiment has dialect and intentional poor spelling throughout, as in Artemas Ward and Petroleum V. Nasby. The opening reads:

GENERAL WILLIS A. GORMAN, ESQ.:

Dere Ole Hoss:—Havin cum down from the Big Woods fer to get eggsemted from the draft, I heerd thar waz a thunderin' big meetin' a goin' to be held in Ingersaul's Haul, in favor uv McClellan, or as the han' bills faseshusly remarked, in favor of McClellan an' the Union. I thaut i'd jist go in an' get squeezed,

as we say poetikally. Little mac is wun uv mi kind of men. Ef
he wuz in kommand i woodent mind the draft, fer they woodent
be no hard marchin' an' not much fitin'. It wood be kam as a
summer's eve.

The letter, occupying almost a full column, goes on to hint
that Gorman profited by cotton speculation in the South, and
it closes by requesting, in return for his support, the post office
at "Le Soor" (Le Sueur).

The remainder of the Minnesota period is of decreasing importance to the making of a realist. Eggleston's stature as a
Minnesotan, and as a Methodist, steadily increased; but his
future was in neither Minnesota nor Methodism. In terms of
general biography, these final years were a time of continued
maturing and of engaging in certain activities that made him,
when he left in 1866, a man of some distinction.

In June, 1863, he acquired a college degree, as unexpected as
it was unearned. The explanation appears in a letter his stepfather wrote just after attending the commencement at Indiana
Asbury: "The Master's degree was conferred upon you with
very general and hearty consent. I hope it will be grateful
to yourself that this honor comes from the best institution in
your native state. The *fee*, I will pay myself, and hope you
will accept it as a very small present."[62]

Eggleston may thus have been in 1863 the only Master of
Arts selling, from door to door, subscriptions to *Headley's History
of the Great Rebellion*, and hoping to average five dollars a
day. The publishers wanted him to add Colton's *Railroad and
County Map of the United States*;[63] instead, he turned in July
to the potentially more lucrative sale of insurance, as state
agent for the Home Life Insurance Company of New York. He
was promised fifteen per cent on all new policies written in the
state and five per cent of all subsequent premiums, and he
was encouraged to pay agents of his choice from five to ten
per cent.[64] Had business and financial profits really attracted
him, he could easily have turned this agency into a great
success; but, as so often before, other interests distracted his
attention and by the end of the year he relegated insurance to
a part-time avocation.

One of these distractions was writing a history of the Sioux
Outbreak. Early in June, 1863, aboard a riverboat near Winona,

he had talked with a friend about such a book, and by the end of the month he had a favorable letter from a publisher.[65] When another Methodist preacher advertised for information about the Outbreak, he felt abused; he was not inclined to step aside, even for a friend.[66] But he never completed his history.[67]

Another distraction was library work. St. Paul had two libraries, supported by the YMCA and the Mercantile Library Association. These merged in October, 1863, as the St. Paul Library Association, the immediate forerunner of the city's public library. Eggleston, who had often urged communities to organize both YMCA's and libraries, attended the first joint meeting and was elected corresponding secretary and librarian. Although St. Paul still honors him as its first librarian, he could not have given much time to the work; by January, 1864, he was "elevated" to the Board of Directors.[68]

A third distraction was the stereopticon. In April, 1863, he had had occasion to help an itinerant showman named Milburn secure bookings,[69] and on occasion he and Milburn traveled together.[70] By February, 1864, Milburn was gone and Eggleston was the showman.[71] On the twelfth, in Minneapolis, he took in $33.00, about half of it profit; on the twenty-third, at St. Anthony, he grossed $15.00; on March 7, at Stillwater, $27.50.[72] But the novelty wore off, and such expenses as new lenses increased. At Hastings on April 1 he collected $22.30 but had to spend $21.00—little better than breaking even.[73] By the eighth his spirits were drooping; for the entire trip he was only $32.00 to the good. He kept running into unavoidable competition—an election in Hastings, a Negro minstrel troupe in Winona. There were other troubles too—a riverboat lodged on a sandbar, noisy inns, headaches from too much coffee. Finally he burnt a hole in the bottom of his retort, had to cancel his show, and decided to sell out.[74]

With more success than enthusiasm, Eggleston turned back to the selling of life insurance. The mere making of money did not appeal to him; the means of making it had to have an intrinsic interest. His reluctance to abandon something he liked to do, such as the stereopticon showings, despite the small financial returns, was matched by his readiness to quit a lucrative occupation that he found uncongenial. Even when, later on, he made a good deal from some of his writing, he never changed his frugal habits, but invested the money, or gave it to his daughters. The only extravagances of his entire life were the modest continuing one of buying books and the costly, occasional one of European travel. Lizzie, tiring of her husband's numerous trips away from home, suggested moving to Chicago to be near her family, but he had a different idea: "Let us go to Europe this summer or next fall." They could sell their real estate; and living was reportedly cheap abroad.[75] But, as it turned out, he had to wait another fifteen years for his first Atlantic crossing.

Lizzie could not have been blamed for feeling jealous, consciously or subconsciously, of the Thomas Simpsons, an important Methodist family of Winona. Eggleston stayed with them often, and he never concealed the fact that he and they were on intimate terms. " 'Zoroaster Higgins' is a brick," Simpson wrote, "better than Artemas Ward. *So says my wife.*"[76] A month later, Eggleston wrote from Winona that Mrs. Simpson wanted to be his amanuensis for his "Winter Evening Book";[77] but by that time the annual Methodist Conference had assigned him to Winona[78] and he was busy supervising the repairs the parsonage needed before his family could join him. In a sentimental mood he described a $10,000 stock farm owned by a dying local man and wondered what kind of estate *he* would leave if he suddenly died.[79]

Chauncey Hobart, an early historian of Methodism in Minnesota, called Eggleston a "prodigy of versatility"[80]—a good phrase to keep in mind when trying to trace the erratic course of his career. By the time of his final pastorate in Minnesota, in Winona from 1864 to 1866, he was an excellent preacher, but preaching was only one of his occupations. He kept up the insurance agency. He was trying his hand at articles, and finished one on George Northrup.[81] He was active in the state Conference, especially in its support of Hamline College. He was an ardent proponent of a state Ministerial Association. But of all his various peripheral activities at this time, the most important and interesting was Eggleston's work for the Northwestern Sanitary Fair; it compensated for his frustrated earlier efforts to help the Northern cause.

The private concerns of all citizens, pressing as they often became, were set against the backdrop of the Civil War. Death was a grim fact: Betty Cocke wrote from Virginia, after a friend was killed, "This is a cruel, cruel war & I pray on bended knee that it may soon cease. . . . We must have been a very wicked people, for the Lord's hand is laid heavily upon us."[82] Hardly less grim were the lengthening lists of the wounded, who taxed the available soldiers' homes and hospitals. At Mrs. Simpson's request, Eggleston investigated in July, 1864, the reported shortage of medical supplies at Fort Snelling; Winona had a surplus that could be sent there.[83] In October, the managers of the Soldiers' Home in Chicago decided to conduct a fair to benefit both the Home and the Sanitary Commission in its work throughout the region.[84] The idea grew rapidly; each nearby state organized its own Commission. In mid-December, Cyrus Bentley of Chicago invited Eggleston to serve as the Commission's agent for Minnesota; an inserted note from Lizzie's brother, William Goodsmith, urged him to accept.[85] Mrs. Simpson, appointed to the committee of the State Commission, no doubt had her own kind of influence; for by March, 1865, Eggleston was co-chairman, along with Governor Stephen Miller, of the Minnesota campaign. Eggleston wrote news releases and also a three-page pamphlet that was distributed throughout the state. It solicited a bushel of wheat from every farmer, cash, Indian relics, and anything else that people might wish to contribute.[86]

In the early months of 1865 he was often in Chicago, meeting people, attending to a thousand details, even preaching a little. The Goodsmiths were delighted with him and hoped he would soon move to Illinois.[87] He also made a good impression on Alfred Sewell, the dynamic chairman of two subcommittees—one on Printing, Blank Books, and Stationery; the other on the Wisconsin War Eagle (a regimental mascot that became a fixture of large fairs for many years to come). Sewell was planning to establish a juvenile magazine named *The Little Corporal* which was destined to become the first Chicago periodical to win national attention and was one of the forerunners of *St. Nicholas*.[88] The Sanitary Fair opened on May 30, ran its course, and yielded its heartening aid to the hospitalized soldiers; but the more important outcome for Eggleston was the series of contributions he made to *The Little Corporal* in almost every monthly issue from August, 1865, until June, 1868.

Sewell and Eggleston had much in common, especially the capacity for big ideas and projects. During the fall of 1865 they corresponded about a campaign to improve orphan asylums;

at one point Sewell spoke of $2,500 as salary if Eggleston would take charge.[89] Sewell also conceived the idea of a Montreal edition of *The Little Corporal* and sounded Eggleston out on moving there to manage it.[90] Both men saw the immense possibilities of Indian stories; Eggleston wrote a good dozen of them for the magazine. He also sent in, at Sewell's urging, rebuses, anecdotes, anagrams, charades, riddles—the *sine qua non* of children's periodicals. The only flaw was that the magazine had no capital and was not yet making money. Its circulation reached 11,000 by December, 1865, but needed about 15,000 to break even; Sewell hoped for 30,000 by the next July.[91] He apologized for the low rate of payment, but in the next breath he suggested a desk job in Chicago and asked Eggleston whether he was a reliable man in money matters.[92] When he learned that Eggleston was hopeful of being appointed consul to Dublin, Sewell foresaw a flow of manuscripts with an Irish flavor. "You are a man after my own heart," he wrote, "& I want you to know how well I appreciate you. . . . With your *brains* and my *drive* we can do something for the little folks worth the doing."[93] With new subscriptions coming in at about a thousand a week, optimism was justified—and Eggleston was pushed closer and closer to a major decision.

Always earlier the question had been merely theoretical— whether to devote his life to religion or to literature. The two goals were no longer, in his mind, so antithetical as they had been when he burnt all his writings and bitterly reproached himself for lack of religious zeal. But he was realistic enough to know that he could not maintain both careers at once with maximum success in either. He sought advice in making the decision, and got it. Terrell wisely asked if the higher salary in Chicago would offset the free parsonage and other perquisites in Winona, but he also admitted that the pastor had to yield to the husband-father.[94] One Methodist colleague viewed the editorial possibility as a bait to draw him from the path of duty, but added: "If you are satisfied that the regular work is your calling, I should advise you to stick to it—if authorship, I should, with my present light, advise you to go."[95] But it was Sewell who tipped the scales: on March 12, 1866, just before leaving for New York to establish an edition there, he dashed off a typically impulsive note: "if I should be killed on the cars I want *you* to adopt my little Corporal, as your own child."[96]

By the end of April the decision was made. Governor Marshall sent his personal regrets that Minnesota was losing Eggleston;[97] but the state's loss was youthful America's gain, if we listen to Sewell: "I have the great pleasure of announcing this month," he wrote in the June issue, "that Edward Eggleston will hereafter share my editorial labors." All who liked the Indian stories would rejoice.[98]

Eggleston went through the motions of requesting superannuation, and remained for some years on the roll of the Minnesota Methodist Conference;[99] he also served as a relief preacher on many occasions; was editor of Sunday school publications; and, in the later 1870's, renewed his ministerial career by accepting a non-denominational pulpit in Brooklyn. But the move to Illinois, in the late spring of 1866, was symbolic of the most important change in direction of a life studded with such changes. Until then, the church had been the center of Eggleston's life; henceforth, the center was writing.

## CHAPTER 3

# Apprenticeship

## I *Writing for Children*

W HEN EGGLESTON MOVED in June, 1866, from Minnesota to Illinois and from preaching to writing, he was twenty-eight years old and had a wife and three daughters to support—the third, Blanche, had been born in September, 1863. As his stepfather had predicted, living costs proved to be higher in Chicago than in St. Paul or in Winona. The new venture called for steady hard work and, as soon as possible, for more sources of income than the somewhat precarious editorial association with *The Little Corporal*. A career in literature, his alternate boyhood dream, was a goal worth whatever effort it would require. He learned, in Illinois, that authorship was a citadel not easily or quickly stormed. It was one that could be won, if at all, only by a long siege, and with a degree of patience and persistence that he had never brought to any of his earlier efforts.

Failure would not have been fatal: he could always return to the pulpit—and he often did—to supplement his income. It is an advantage clergymen have over most other people, partly because sermons are usually delivered on Sunday, a day when most other professional activity is suspended. In former years, Eggleston had sought to supplement a meager clerical salary by selling soap or books or insurance; now, an occasional sermon was a prop in lean times, an insurance against disaster, a trump card he could play over and over again. In his ambition to be a writer, however, the all-important consideration was keeping the pulpit in the secondary place he had now assigned to it.

He had also discovered that he could make money by lecturing. The easy flow of language which, as a youngster, he had often considered a moral flaw that he prayed for the power to suppress, he now accepted as an asset that could be exploited. Not every effective preacher is an equally effective lecturer; Eggleston had the good fortune to be both. In December, 1866, he made a lecture tour of Minnesota; his topic was "Pembina," a congenial reworking of his trip with the eclipse expedition in 1860. "My welcome in Winona & St. Paul," he wrote his wife, "has been of the most flattering kind."[1] The St. Paul *Press* remarked that "He never yet failed to amuse and interest an audience."[2] By the twentieth he had cleared more than $150 and was confident of doubling that sum by New Year's; it was the most he had ever earned with so little effort.

It was also a rate of income higher than he was enjoying as associate editor of *The Little Corporal*. With no capital reserves the magazine kept alive on a month-to-month basis, using the money that came in for new subscriptions. These continued to be fairly numerous, but Alfred Sewell kept adjusting upward the circulation figure that would be needed to break even. For Eggleston, acceptance of this reality meant a continued deferring of the larger salary that Sewell, in his moments of visionary optimism, had honestly hoped could be paid. It was soon obvious to Eggleston, whose own financial reserves were no better than the magazine's, that *The Little Corporal* merely provided a toehold on literature; to gain a solid footing he would have to do more.

Almost at once, accordingly, he communicated with other editors. Sometimes they wrote first: J. W. Daughaday, for example, wrote at least three letters from Philadephia soliciting Indian yarns for the *School Visitor*.[3] More often Eggleston wrote first, as unestablished authors are usually forced to do. He sent his George Northrup article to the Harper firm, which forwarded it to Ticknor and Fields, publishers of *Our Young Folks*.[4] The latter found it unusual, but also unusable, and sent it back to *Harper's*.[5] The editors doubted its authenticity[6] but accepted it; then they laid it aside and did not print it until 1894 when it appeared with the title "The-Man-that-Draws-the-Handcart."[7] That such a magazine would be interested in the article was an incentive, even if the long delay in publication was a frustration. Of much more immediate value was a promise from *Harper's* to accept any factual reports of up to 15,000 words apiece that he might write about places he visited and to pay fees ranging from twenty-five to thirty dollars.[8] These reports, at about a fifth of a cent per word, can only be called hack work; but Eggleston welcomed the chance, since it roughly doubled his earnings on his Minnesota lecture trip.

Such a trip, lasting a good month, was possible because he had little trouble keeping ahead of his *Little Corporal* assignments—even when he composed entire issues. To conceal this fact of single authorship, he resorted to a multiple set of pseudonyms: Ease and E. Square, for his initials; Captain Jack; Professor Willie; Private Queer; Pease and Cues; Keystone; Clef de Voute. His best writing for the magazine was a group of Indian narratives in the two series "Round Table Stories" and "Evenings at the Nest." Eggleston's extensive wanderings in Minnesota had given him a wide store of knowledge about the Indians that he could now draw upon; in addition, he had the material he had collected for an unfinished book about the Sioux Outbreak of 1862. He repeatedly stressed the factual accuracy of every incident; even for juvenile readers he avoided the romanticizing that had made Longfellow's *Song of Hiawatha* a best-seller in 1855. In that poem Hiawatha, a Chippewa, marries Minnehaha, a girl from the enemy Dakotas (or Sioux); in one of his stories Eggleston has a listener interrupt the narrative to express shocked disbelief that the massacres of 1862 were committed by men of Minnehaha's tribe. "They were," was the reply, "for you must learn, my dear little enthusiast, that the Indians the poets write about are very different from the wild and brutal savages themselves."[9]

This attitude toward the Indians reflects the literalness of Eggleston's boyhood and was a good augur of the realism of his later writing. But his progress toward uncompromising realism was not so straightforward as this might suggest. In July, 1866, a story he had translated from the French of Hendrick Conscience, "The Antwerp Laborer and His Family," appeared in *The Ladies' Repository*.[10] The plot is simple: one wealthy girl initiates another into the joys of helping the worthy poor. It is impossible to ignore, or to explain away, the basic insipidity of the situation, which was not a thing he could get rid of in the process of translating. The fact that he would be sufficiently attracted to the original to want to do a translation betrays the same kind of sentimentality that various contemporary critics deplored in his first novels. On the other hand, this preoccupation with lowly people—a laborer's family—foreshadows the simple characters in humble circumstance that are almost exclusively the human subjects of his novels. His next story of this "literary" sort—again a translation but this time from the Italian—was "The Unfortunate Widow" (January, 1867).[11] Of the great mass of weekly writing between then and the appearance of *The Hoosier School-Master* late in 1871, only two or three titles are of consciously literary attempts—and in all of them this sentimentality is present. Drawing upon frontier actualities yielded a laudable degree of realism; trying to be "literary" did not.

If the labored "literary" efforts represent an advance in no useful direction, and even a detour of positive harm to his career, the necessity of filling up each issue of *The Little Corporal* had only slightly greater value. The rebuses, conundrums, and anecdotes, if he devised them all, reflect an inventive capacity approaching genius; some of the puzzles were of an intricacy to command the full attention of child prodigies. It is probable, however, that he borrowed or adapted some of his material from the numerous volumes of jokes and puzzles then in circulation, for it is hard to credit him with total originality, month after month. Yet the word play that was at the heart of many of his "fillers" apparently had a genuine fascination for him; it appears in a different form in his novels. A special kind of playfulness, the exact opposite of realism, introduced the supernatural, as in "Lazy Larkin and the Joblilies." Supernaturalism also recurred in the novels, especially in *The Circuit Rider*, in which two mysterious dogs appear from nowhere and accompany the heroine on a long night ride, and a white dove alights on a dying man's breast.

Another and more important link between the magazine and his later career is a pattern of development common to both the Indian stories and the novels: as one Eggleston scholar puts it, "a discursive plot with inadequately assimilated moralizing or playful digressions."[12] The habit can even be traced back to the sermons, which were not close-knit in logical unity. His typical sermon, in bare outline, consisted of an exordium from scripture, topical variations, and practical suggestions. A pattern common in his fiction is roughly parallel: introduction of a quotation or generalization, application to a current situation, and a conclusion showing the interaction of the two. The middle terms are the ingredients in common: both reflect his meditations, his thinking based on recent reading and observation, and both offered an opportunity for discursiveness and apparent irrelevance.

The element of playfulness, common to the early stories and the novels, and the three-step structural device common to both of these and also to the sermons, are major parts of the internal evidence, if such were needed, that the same man wrote them all.[13]

## II  *New Deadlines*

In December, 1866, Eggleston was appointed editor of *The Sunday School Teacher,* at a beginning salary of $1,000 a year— a very welcome addition to his income. Earlier he had contributed occasional Sunday school lessons for a flat fee; now each week he wrote the lead editorial and presumably the "Editor's Table." The publishers, Adams, Blackmer & Lyon, also brought out separate handbooks that Eggleston wrote: *Sunday-School Conventions and Institutes* (1867), *Improved Sunday-School Record* and *The Manual: A Practical Guide to the Sunday-School Work* (both in 1869), and *Tracts for Sunday School Teachers* (1870). The Sunday school movement was about a century old: Robert Raikes, in England, was the pioneer. The first American Sunday school (so labeled) was organized in 1795 in Virginia by Bishop Asbury, who also instituted the Circuit Rider system. By 1824 the movement became interdenominational; but the Methodists remained its strongest supporters, and Eggleston's new position was a logical outcome of his career in the Methodist pulpit.

The lead articles that he wrote as editor were practical and were directed to Sunday school workers. Typical titles were "The Teacher's General Preparation," "Choosing a Superintendent," and "A Few Words to the Superintendent." Whatever their value to the profession, they provided a steady week-to-week means of acquiring readiness in composition. Another weekly exercise, beginning at the same time—late in 1866—was a series of unsigned essays that he wrote for the Chicago *Evening Journal* under the general title "Our Saturday Feuilleton."[14] With all due respect to the Sunday school as an institution, this newspaper column was much more interesting than his increasingly authoritative advice to the adults responsible for religious instruction—and much more important to the development of his realism.

If these *Journal* essays were to be collected, the volume would be a valuable portrait of ordinary life in Chicago just after the Civil War. Instead of recalling what he had learned about Indians on the frontier for a juvenile audience or of laboriously translating sentimental stories in an effort to be literary, he simply recorded what he saw in the city, day and night: streetcars, newsboys, signs, handbills and posters, dogs, bridges, servant girls. A *feuilleton* is a part of a French newspaper devoted to light literature; and Eggleston was loyal to this meaning. "Life in the Street Cars," dated November 17, 1866, and the first in the series, is a good example. Despite the crowding and other discomforts, Eggleston liked the cars, finding them a greater leveler than books or graves; as a leveler, he wrote, the grave is "nothing to a South Side car on a rainy night." Humanity in all its variety is thrown together; distinctions are stripped away. A Negro girl sits down by a Southerner, who rises and retreats to the platform. A boy yields his seat to a gawdy wench—an example of misplaced gallantry as long as a tired washerwoman remains standing. Conversations struck up with strangers could be dangerous; for Eggleston tells of inveighing against a certain monopoly only to learn that his auditor was its ex-president and founder.

The *feuilleton* essays were good potential background for a fictional treatment of Chicago—if Eggleston had seen fit to use them in that way. The only "story line," a very thin one, is the author's week-by-week contact with the manifold actuality of the city. The inchoate rambling that the medium encouraged was one more formative influence on his novels; if not confirming his tendency to discursiveness, at least it did not correct it.

By March, 1867, Eggleston felt sufficiently established in lecturing and other work to resign his editorial position on *The Little Corporal.* He had become editor in name only, he explained; and, besides, Sewell was restored to full health and could carry on alone.[15] As if to illustrate the point, Eggleston spent most of March in Indiana, lecturing in Indianapolis, Greensburgh, New Albany, and elsewhere. Absence from home always brought out the sentimental in his nature. On March 18, for example, he remembered the day nine years before when he and Lizzie had been married: "If I have done anything, or shall ever do anything of value in the world it will be due, under God, to the strength I have received from your sympathy & counsel."[16] On the twenty-second, in Greencastle, he reported: "Have been a great deal lionized & petted."[17] His lecture there barely paid his expenses, but that afternoon he was initiated into Phi Gamma Delta; like his honorary master's degree, fraternity membership was another link to the college (now DePauw) that he would have attended if his father's wise foresight had prevailed.[18] At New Albany his audience was better, but a local paper made sport of his lecture —to his chagrin.[19] In Madison he visited a cousin, Mack Goode, and enjoyed perusing the commonplace book of his former mentor, Guilford Eggleston. His final lecture, in Vevay, was the climax of this return to the past—a return he repeated fairly often in his final decades.

During 1867 the Chicago *Tribune* waged an aggressive campaign to improve prisons and poor-houses, which were generally in a worse condition than they had been before the Civil War. In June, Eggleston joined the crusade with a detailed report about Freeport, Illinois.[20] The jail, he wrote—under one of his *Little Corporal* pen-names, Clef de Voute—made the Black Hole of Calcutta seem a paradise, while the Stephenson County Poor House suffered the all too common fault of not classifying and segregating the various inmates. The saddest mental case was not in an institution: a wealthy citizen of Freeport, he learned, had for thirteen years been keeping his harmless lunatic daughter in a small stone house, six feet square, solely to save the cost of putting her in an asylum. A stranger in Springfield wrote to applaud the article and to urge Eggleston to look at the public institutions in La Salle County.[21] But his next such article was about Davenport, Iowa,[22] where he found more filth and disorder than was usual in such places; idiots and simple-minded children were lodged in the same quarters as lewd women rotting with disesase. The humanitarian impulse these two articles reflect was to come to light again in *The Hoosier School-Master* and was to lead reviewers to suggest a parallel to Dickens.

In the late fall Eggleston went east, attending conventions and speaking on Sunday school matters at Washington, Baltimore, and Brooklyn. "My trip East," he wrote his wife, "has been a perfect tour of conquest"—so successful that John Heyl Vincent, a national leader in Sunday school work, had to caution him to "keep humble."[23]

It was good to meet such men as Vincent, men whose published opinions he respected and whose good opinion he valued. Vincent subsequently extended his activities to the Chautauqua movement, and on one occasion he enlisted Eggleston's help, for a substantial fee. One other man met on this trip, Henry Bowen, proprietor of *The Independent*, had a more immediate economic bearing on Eggleston's career. The previous October he had begun accepting weekly letters from Eggleston which were printed as "Our Western Correspondence" and signed "Penholder." Bowen, evidently impressed by the letters and then by their author, spoke, though vaguely, about putting him on a fixed salary. The letters had a threefold value for Eggleston: as the source of a welcome increment to income, as practice in a kind of writing different from other work and meant for a liberal intellectual audience, and as good preparation for his eventual staff position on *The Independent*. In addition to the regular letters, he contributed occasional special reports of such events as the Republican National Convention, the Methodist General Conference, the YMCA International Convention, the National Sunday-School Convention, and the Woman's Suffrage Convention. These suggest, in the composite, a catholic interest in group meetings and a willingness to sit through many long sessions.

## III  *Shady Evanston*

The novelty of big city life, reflected in the "Saturday Feuilleton" essays, did not last; Eggleston soon gravitated to suburban Evanston, a Methodist stronghold as the seat of Northwestern University and a village not too unlike his native Vevay, or Stillwater, or Winona. He could do much of his weekly writing at home, and ride the train into Chicago only when he had to. Increasingly, as his Sunday school reputation grew, Chicago represented only the point of departure to other cities—to Kalamazoo, East Saginaw, and Owasso in Michigan; to Plainfield and Newark in New Jersey; to Brooklyn, Philadelphia, New York, Troy; and to Wilmington, Delaware. Since he wrote to his wife only on these trips, his letters give the somewhat misleading impression that he was more often away than at home; homebody that he was, he was never quite able to dispel the sense of loneliness in these periods of separation. And Evanston grew on him: "How I wish I were back again in shady Evanston!"[24] His sister Jennie, whose rather aimless wanderings had been a source of concern to him, married the Reverend Charles H. Zimmerman and settled in Evanston—one more reason for thinking of the lakeshore village as a permanent home.

It was a heady experience being invited to speak in distant cities, to conduct institutes for Sunday school staffs, and to be asked for his opinion as a professional. He established, in his Evanston home, one of the country's first kindergartens, which automatically broadened his reputation as an expert. This accretion to fame was a principal reason for his first visit to New England in September, 1869; there the extremely friendly welcome, the enforced quiet on Sunday, the beautiful scenery, and the thriftiness obvious everywhere made him, for once, forget to be lonely when away from home.[25]

The post-Civil War period, which is often viewed as a tragic era or as a gilded age, was, for most Americans, a time of great stimulation and release of energy as individuals became absorbed in reshaping virtually every institution within the civilization. Men like Eggleston—ambitious, restless, and versatile—had little trouble finding things to do and ways to do them. The culture was ready for them, welcomed their contributions, kept them busy, and provided the warming sense of sharing in vast new enterprises. Eggleston's total output, in words spoken and written, from 1866 until his death in 1902, was prodigious; and it was of recognized value in a number of human activities. In 1869, at the age of thirty-one, he may have been simply too busy to ask himself whether what he was doing was what he wanted to do.

The four years in Illinois, from the spring of 1866 to the spring of 1870, had brought him far; the precarious toehold had become a firm footing. But it was not, as he had hoped, a solid footing in literature. Four short children's stories in *Little Corporal* comprise his entire creative output in 1868 and 1869.

Even the essays for the "Saturday Feuilleton" had stopped in the fall of 1867. Instead of gaining on literature, he was rapidly losing ground; his growing reputation was rather in journalism and religious education. No diary survives for this period to reveal what misgivings may have hidden behind the facade of success; but his letters show an increasing self-confidence, an achieved maturity, and a zest for life that circumstance had never quite permitted earlier. For the moment, at least, the solid awareness of recognition banished the morbid soul-searching that had severely limited his boyhood happiness and that had made his early manhood a time of indecision and frustration.

Evanston was increasingly a good place to live and a good base for the travels that his reputation encouraged. New York remained a possibility, but hardly more. *The Independent* seemed willing enough to add his name to its editorial roster; but he was a virtual non-resident staff member already, without having to give up the good life in Evanston. If, in 1866, he had thought of Illinios as a mere way station on the route to better things, it was not that now; it was home, increasingly beloved every year.

But even the strongest emotional ties are sometimes broken. Early in 1870 he received, and accepted, a concrete offer for an office position with *The Independent*. One important reason for going was a tragic one—the death of his only son, Edward William, on November 4, 1869, in his fourth year. His birth on May 29, 1866, had almost exactly coincided with the move to Illinois. Evanston suddenly lost much of its savor; Eggleston could leave it now without too great reluctance.

The loss may have jolted Eggleston into remembering former ambitions. In glancing over some papers not long after his son's death, he came across the list of Hoosier terms he had jotted down in February, 1863, and on an impulse sent it off to James Russell Lowell, whose literary use of Yankee speech gave dialect a stamp of approval. Lowell's reply, dated January 19, 1870, was cordial and encouraging. "Remember," said Lowell, "that it will soon be too late. Railways are mixing and the school-master rooting-out." But he added that mere recording of local dialect, however valuable to the science of language, had never been his own prime concern, "for you must remember that Mr Biglow was not writing to illustrate a dialect—but using his lingo as a cudgel."

Such a letter is stronger encouragement than most literary hopefuls ever get. Dialect, not as an end in itself as in a scholar's list, but used as a cudgel—what was this if not a challenge to authorship? To ignore the challenge would have been a cowardly withdrawal, an evasion of duty, a final abandonment of the literary impulse that was not dead but was being smothered by reams of the journalistic writing that was supposedly the means of approaching literature. Lowell's letter revived the urgency; what remained for Eggleston was the question *How?*

## IV  *Back-Trailing Completed*

The move from Minnesota to Illinois in 1866 was made with the deliberate intention of exchanging a preacher's career for a writer's. The next move, to New York in 1870, the final step in back-trailing, was in comparison only a slight readjustment in course. Instead of mailing weekly contributions to *The Independent,* Eggleston turned out weekly assignments at his desk in its editorial offices at 2 Park Row near the lower tip of Manhattan Island. The change did affect his relations with the *National Sunday School Teacher,*[26] however; his editorials soon dwindled to zero, although he contributed occasional articles for several more years.

As a kind of parting salute, his Chicago publishers made Eggleston's first year in New York a banner year for him by publishing four of his books. Two were related to his Sunday school work: *Tracts for Sunday School Teachers,* and *The Infant Class* by Sara J. Timanus, which he edited and provided with an introduction. The other two represent his alternate impulse, the one toward literature: *Book of Queer Stories and Stories Told on a Cellar Door* and *Mr. Blake's Walking Stick.* The first of these had the misfortune of being destroyed, plates and all, in the Chicago Fire of 1871;[27] but it was obviously a selection of his stories in *The Little Corporal.* The second, which he dedicated to the memory of his son,[28] runs to fifty pages. The division into eleven chapters gives it the superficial appearance of being a novelette, but the slimness of the volume itself accurately reflects the thin quality of the story.

The walking stick, of solid ebony with a boxwood head carved in the likeness of an old man, serves its owner, Mr. Blake, as a companion on his pastoral rounds in the village of Thornton. Shortly before Christmas, Blake's thirteen-year-old son Willie imagines a conversation with the walking stick, which recommends two Bible verses, Luke 14: 12-13; by a neat coincidence these serve as text for Blake's sermon the next Sunday. Willie has recently become aware of certain local families with distressing financial troubles, and the verses, advocating aid to the needy, prompt him to a course of direct action. He cajoles his classmates, first in his Sunday school and during the week in public school, to exchange their usual idle curiosity about the Christmas presents they hope to receive for effective group efforts to reduce their neighbors' distress. His own class, by various means, manages to buy the sewing machine that will save Widow Martin from binding out her oldest son and daughter. The climactic scene is the discomfiting of Lampeer, the hardhearted overseer of the poor, at the very moment when Widow Martin, in desperation, is about to sign the fatal papers. Lampeer is a caricature but he no doubt fairly represented the compassion. At the Christmas party in the Sunday school, all of Thornton's needy are guests of honor—the impoverished elders, the orphaned young, the blind, the crippled, even the idiots; all of them have been specifically helped in the campaign begun by Willie at the instigation of his father's walking stick.

The story, sentimental and improbable though it is, has certain relationships to contemporary thinking and practice. Lampeer's opinion that "everybody that was poor was rascally" mirrors the orthodox complacency of dominant Protestantism in the 1870's, which in general equated economic failure with essential depravity. Binding out children was not so common as earlier in the nineteenth century, but Eggleston clearly hoped to accelerate its decline; in *The Hoosier School-Master* he made the heroine a bound-girl. The entire concept of public welfare, so greatly expanded since 1870, was as primitive and unenlightened as Eggleston pictured it in this story and also in his muckraking contributions, a little earlier, to the Chicago *Tribune*. Lampeer is a caricature but he no doubt fairly represented the kind of man commonly entrusted with administering the limited aid that the taxpayers then provided. This point is less explicit in the story, however, than the exposure of greedy Tommy Puffer who, alone among the children, fails to share in the pleasure of giving—a frontal attack on the vice of selfishness.

The collected stories and *Mr. Blake's Walking Stick* were a declaration of intent that Eggleston was soon in a position to follow up; but he was not so consumed with impatience that he slighted his staff work on *The Independent*. His initial assignment was as book editor. After five months he was promoted and, as superintending editor, directed the editorial policy, but his opinions about current literature have a greater relevance to an inquiry into his development as a writer.

If he could speak with authority on any one literary genre, it was on books for boys, since he was an old hand at juvenile writing. Most books of this sort he scornfully dismissed. *Roy's Search, Hopedale Tavern*, and similar temperance novels were too exciting and harrowing, he thought, for young minds.[29] He also rejected the Sabbath story: "Three parts of religion to ninety-seven parts swash," he remarked, "make a first rate Sunday-School book." *Robinson Crusoe, Tom Brown's School Days*, and *Sandford and Merton* were greatly to be preferred.[30] Among the very worst offenders were such "get-rich" stories as the "Oliver Optic" series, "the most successful corrupter of youth in America."[31] The one American juvenile writer whom he could praise without reservation was Jacob Abbott, who had "never written a bad book, a dull book, or a book that was not elevating in its influence."[32]

On other literary subjects Eggleston was often less assured and sometimes myopic in his values. A volume of poems by Bret Harte prompted an essay on western slang;[33] he already knew what has since become accepted knowledge—that Posey County, Indiana, and Pike County, Missouri, were the two chief sources of the colorful language later made famous by Mark Twain. He went astray, however, in ranking Harte second only to Lowell as a poet of characterization and in preferring a poem by Helen Hunt to Twain's column in the *Galaxy*. He was correct enough, however, in his opinion about Bayard Taylor: "he will not be our great American novelist."[34]

Some of Eggleston's critical opinions (if brief and often perfunctory comments can pass as criticism) were no doubt more expressive of contemporary standards than of his considered judgment—his objection, for example, to Charles Reade's coarseness. In these weekly remarks, however, and until the 1890's, he showed a consistent coolness toward French realism, on moral grounds; the English Channel, in separating British and French literary taste and behavior, was as wide, he once observed, as the Atlantic Ocean.[35] But he was also quick to defend American writing against any adverse criticism from British sources. When in November, 1870, the pro-American *Westminster Review* ventured a general estimate of American writers, he set about correcting its judgments. Of the poets singled out for attention— Longfellow, Poe, Nathaniel Parker Willis, Whitman, and Whittier —he rejected Poe and Willis as minor in importance and Whitman as scarcely known at all. The *Review* had erred grievously, he thought, in not mentioning our greatest authors—Irving, Hawthorne, and Lowell.[36]

Such opinions, which may be taken as typical of Eggleston's professional thinking for the *Independent,* offer slight promise of a notable new departure in American literature within the next year. Sound enough on books for children, he was considerably more conservative than William Dean Howells, like himself, a westerner who had moved east and a journalist ambitious to become a writer. Howells had no ministerial background to exert a lingering moralistic influence; in addition, his four-year visit to Europe during the Civil War gave him the advantage of a cosmopolitan outlook. Eggleston's low opinion of Twain (the extreme opposite of Howells' very high one) is hard to reconcile with the warm praise he accorded to Harte and to others, including Phoebe Cary, who helped put the west into literature. He saw in Harte, Hay, and Howells "the beginnings of a race of men who will do justice to the customs and speech of the west"; Twain he pointedly omitted from this list.[37] He never could fully appreciate Twain, and he referred to him privately in 1888 as "only a good clown after all."[38] Josh Billings drew his admiration; so did *Sam Lawson's Oldtown Fireside Stories* by Harriet Beecher Stowe; so also did Rebecca Harding Davis' "Life in the Iron Mills," one of the true pioneers of realism. The fact that he applauded it cannot be taken as evidence of a significant leaning toward realism, however; if any leaning is discernible, it was toward regionalism, whether realistic or romantic.

Among the foreign writers Eggleston had occasion to mention were Arnold, Ruskin, Lamb, Huxley, Dickens, Goldsmith, George Sand, Friedrich Spielhagen, and George MacDonald. The experience of this general reading was an intensive renewal of his boyhood bookishness, with the important difference that

religious scruples no longer kept him from fiction, as something
not true. He reviewed all kinds of books—whatever the publishers
submitted. If his ambition to become a novelist had taken firm
shape, he might have shown a preference for fiction; but even
though he didn't, it is improper to say that when he wrote *The
Hoosier School-Master* he was unread in the novel.

Eggleston went to *The Independent* at a critical time in its
history. Henry Ward Beecher, its original editor-in-chief, and
Theodore Tilton, currently in charge, were at loggerheads; so
were Joshua Leavitt, the religious editor, and William Lloyd
Garrison, a leading contributor. In both quarrels the issue was
love and marriage. Henry Bowen, the proprietor, who was already
estranged from Beecher's Plymouth Church, objected to Tilton's
editorial radicalism and feared it might in time hurt the circulation. Late in 1870 Bowen forced Tilton to resign, became
editor-in-chief himself, and appointed mild-tempered Eggleston
as superintending editor, a post he held about eight months,
the climax of his career in journalism.[39]

Prior to this change in status Eggleston had begun to contribute to the editorial page such things as "The Trial of Dr.
Lanahan," "Death of the Dean of Canterbury," "France Delivered!," "Charles Sumner's Removal," "An Evening at Dr. Ormis-
ton's." After his promotion, he assumed the primary responsibility
for lead editorials and left book reviewing to others on the staff.
A commendable desire to broaden the geographic base of contributions, and to improve their quality, took him twice to
Boston, once in January, 1871, and again in February. But
storming the country's literary citadel was not easy. Longfellow
wasn't at home; his reply to a written invitation was polite but
not encouraging:

Cambridge Feb 13
1871

My Dear Sir,
    If I were writing for periodicals, I should accept with pleasure
your handsome offer. But I do very little in that way now, and
that little I feel bound to give to my old friend Mr. Fields for
his magazine.
    Regretting that I am obliged to decline your friendly
proposition,

Yours truly,
Henry W. Longfellow

*[ 83 ]*

Lowell, who *was* at home when Eggleston called and who in any case was an old acquaintance through correspondence, wrote much more warmly:

> Elmwood, 4th March, 1871

My dear Sir,

I have not yet been able to do anything for the "Independent," but I have not forgotten my promise, & will fulfill it as soon as I can.

I am much obliged for your further contribution to my museum of *patois*, & hope, if you pick up any more specimens of which we can possess each other by exchange or duplicates, you will remember me.

I recollect your visit with as much pleasure as you are good enough to express on your own part. . . .

> Very truly yours
> J R Lowell

In yet another letter written in April, Lowell spoke of business matters occupying his time: "But I will engage myself to you for something in June. I shall be in a writing mood again so soon as my present flurry is over."[40] Eggleston was more successful with such New Yorkers as Alice Cary, who sent a "semistory" with Poe as the center of interest,[41] and with Bryant, who submitted a sixty-eight-line excerpt from his almost completed translation of the *Odyssey*.[42]

In addition to possible contributors, Eggleston, as editor, met various personages currently in the news. He found it exhilarating, for example, to interview Charles Sumner in Washington and to become privy to the inner reasons for his break with U. S. Grant and Hamilton Fish.[43] But Eggleston was more excited over a note from William Dean Howells praising a story of his as "a very unaffected bit of good work."[44]

## V  *Short-Story Writing*

The story Howells liked was "Huldah the Help: A Thanksgiving Story," published in the first issue of *Scribner's Monthly* (November, 1870). Eggleston had protested that he had no time to write fiction and, besides, had never tried such writing; but Richard Watson Gilder was so insistent that he complied.

Like some of the Indian tales in *Little Corporal,* "Huldah the
Help" has a plot within a plot: Judge Balcom, after Thanksgiving dinner, is persuaded to tell the story of Huldah, a family
maid who marries the son of the family; at the close, the judge
reveals that he was that son and his wife that maid.

Howells' term "unaffected" suits the story well. A more sophisticated age might prefer other adjectives: artless, amateurish,
commonplace, perhaps even clumsy. But its very simplicity and
lack of artificial complication were refreshing—and *Scribner's*
demanded more of the same. Eggleston supplied four others:
"The Story of a Valentine" printed in February, 1871; "Ben: A
Story for May-Day," in the May issue; "The Gunpowder Plot,"
in July; and "Priscilla," in November. The first closely resembles
"Huldah," for a narrator, the young Reverend Hubert Lee,
tells Dr. Hood, an elderly radical, of two lovers so bashful that
they communicate only through valentines. Lee suggests that
the girl may have been too forward; Hood defends her behavior
and, to be consistent, must give his consent when he learns that
his own daughter is the girl concerned, and Lee her suitor.

The device of an inner story was easy to overuse, and was
hardly one to base a literary career upon. The other three in this
series for *Scribner's* have the special interest of being drawn
from Eggleston's personal recollections. "Ben: A Story for May-
Day" pairs off a "bound boy" and a Swiss girl at the annual
spring frolic in an Indiana village that is obviously Vevay. In
it Eggleston is realistic enough to report that onions have replaced grapes as the basis of the local economy. "Priscilla" is
even more nostalgic: he describes the village, New Geneva, as
"that dearest old-fogy Ohio River village . . . our pleasant town
of vineyards." This story is unusual for Eggleston because it has a
tragic ending; the heroine dies of tuberculosis before she can
decide which of two suitors to accept.

Many of the elements found in these stories about Indiana
were to recur in the novels: popular pastimes, local customs,
regional speech, and the triumph of humble virtue over false
arrogance. Eggleston was never able to recall with equal skill
and assurance the distinguishing qualities of the Minnesota
frontier. His one Minnesota novel, *The Mystery of Metropolisville,* is the closest to autobiography but it does not convey the
authoritative sense of probability. Few individuals had seen so
much of early Minnesota, yet even his extensive knowledge could

not guarantee writing effectively about the place and time.

"The Gunpowder Plot" foreshadows the difficulty he would later have with *Metropolisville*. His own dissatisfaction is reflected in one editorial aside within the story: "Whenever one writes with photographic exactness of frontier life, he is accused of inventing improbable things." Vevay, Indiana, was not so different from villages in the older east that readers would reject it; the Lindsleyville of "The Gunpowder Plot," in contrast, was a single house on the open prairie, a stop on the Red River Trail, a place of incredible loneliness, and much more remote from civilization and from readers' ready acceptance than any of the other settings he used. It was the raw primordial setting for human probing into the wilderness, at the dawn of the process of settlement.

The girl in the story has little to do but watch the geese, the pelicans, and the bald eagles. When strangers come, they are usually Sioux Indians or half-breed voyageurs. The settlers of several embryo counties, gathering for Fourth of July revels, are a motley lot: a few Germans, fewer Yankees, some French Canadians, a retired stage driver named Whiskey Jim, and a state senator skilled in buncombe oratory. The plot is even more outlandish. The hero uses stereopticon slides of the Virgin and the Devil, projected on the side of the one house, to foil a whiskey-engendered plot against Lindsley, the heroine's misanthropic father. Eggleston here drew upon his experience as a stereopticon showman.

The double gratification of seeing these stories in print—and in so good a magazine—and of being urged by its editors to keep on writing them was a strong stimulant to Eggleston's desire to become an author. So strong was his resurgence of literary ambition that in July he resigned his position on the *Independent* to become editor-in-chief of *Hearth and Home,* a family weekly on the verge of extinction. The proprietors, Orange, Judd & Co., specialized in farm publications, including *The American Agriculturist;* but their wish to avoid a loss on *Hearth and Home,* which they had recently bought, was greater than their loyalty to their rural clientele, and they did not object when Eggleston got rid of the pictures of plows and suppressed the horticulture section. They gave him, in fact, a completely free hand. One of his first acts was to hire his brother George away from the Brooklyn *Daily Union*. It was the one time in their lives when their careers thus merged, and they made the most of it. For George it meant a much better job than any he had ever found; for Edward, an associate he could rely on completely; for both of them it was a chance to renew the intimacy of their boyhood and to exchange yarns about the years of their separation and the very different paths they had taken.[45]

But neither the challenge of reviving a dying periodical, nor the opportunity to give his brother a welcome boost, weighed quite so much with Eggleston as the possibility of getting more of his own fiction into print. It wasn't a new idea; he had worked it before in *Little Corporal*, only to exhaust his literary invention by providing virtually all the copy. But the five years since then had greatly altered his circumstances. He was no longer a raw recruit from the remote frontier, volunteering for service in which he had had no prior experience; instead, he was a seasoned campaigner with many thousands of words behind him and with short fiction currently being bought, published, read— and praised by such a man as William Dean Howells. He wasted little time implementing his plan: the first issue of *Hearth and Home* to carry any of his writing, on August 19, 1871, carried the initial installment of "Uncle Sim's Boy."

The story ran for two more installments. On August 26 an editorial comment by Eggleston, "The Reign of the Story," defended fiction against narrow moralistic critics; evidently some reader had submitted a protest. Since this story ended its serial run just four weeks before the first installment of *The Hoosier School-Master*, it may be useful to examine the plot in detail. It offers even fewer hints of the literary sensation just ahead than his recent stories in *Scribner's*. Simeon Harvey, the "Sim" of the title, is the bachelor owner of a Brooklyn Heights boarding house. He assumes the responsibility, with some misgivings, for his orphan nephew Dick, an impetuous youngster who promptly incurs the hostility of the servants by his utter frankness. Uncle Sim, going to Washington on business, leaves both Dick and Jane, his nurse, with his fiancée, wealthy Amelia Cobb. Dick's old habits continue; he soon antagonizes the Cobb servants by insisting on speaking the truth. When he catches the housekeeper's daughter stealing silk, he reports it; but the theft is charged to Jane, who is punished by being discharged. Amelia refuses to listen to Dick, who thereupon leaves the house, wanders the streets until a policeman finds him and takes him, in a feverish condition, to the home of his former music teacher, Miss Mayhew. Uncle Sim returns, and, while helping Miss Mayhew nurse Dick through his fever, he falls in love with her, and marries her, after giving Amelia time to break their engagement. The honeymooners take Dick along on their wedding trip to the Adirondacks to complete his convalesence.

Eggleston was living in Brooklyn when he wrote this story; it is hardly possible to quarrel with the realism of his local setting or, since the race is all but extinct, with his portrayal of household servants. Dick is carefully described as being not a model boy; but his deadly literalness (like Eggleston's own, years earlier) makes him something of a monster, and readers may be tempted to side with the servants. The one character suggestive of a type Eggleston later used frequently in his novels is Amelia, a caricature of amiability uncomplicated by either virtues or vices. Her loss of Sim to a penniless but virtuous music-teacher provides just the sentimental, satisfying outcome that *Hearth and Home* readers no doubt wanted. Whatever faults subsequent judgment may find with Eggleston, he did have the knack of producing what pleased the generality of contemporary middle-class readers. What saves him from mediocrity is the fact that this knack was not confined to the writing of such shadowy, unconvincing, insipid stories as "Uncle Sim's Boy."

As editor, however, Eggleston had to devote a certain number of hours to editorial essays—four or five in each issue—which were topical, varied, and somewhat lighter in tone than his recent writing for the *Independent*. Their evidence indicates that he was enjoying himself. He also revived Zoroaster Higgins as a mouthpiece for a series of impertinent rhymed comments upon such topics as the grafting of the Tweed Ring, Commodore Vanderbilt's guilt in a steamboat disaster, a suicide report from Long Beach that turned out to be a hoax, and Whitman's latest poem. Tweed's flight prompted the following, typical of the others:

> Adieu! immortal Boss, adieu!
> (From the treasury they'll nail you out!)
> Poor Hall will feel the loss of you,
> (Barnard no more will bail you out!)

O'Conor's given goss to you,
    (And made you jibe your sail about!)
The papers all were cross to you,
    (Your sureties all turned tail about!)
The city knows the cost of you,
    (That's what the people rail about!)
A farewell kick they toss to you,
    (You should have gone to jail, you lout!)
Oh! lying, stealing Boss, adieu![46]

Eggleston also invented a new pen-name, "The Leisurely Saunterer," for a lengthy series of essays in *Hearth and Home*. Relaxed and genial, ranging over a great many subjects, these essays are his "Saturday Feuilleton" grown older, more mature and mellow, and more interesting. Typical titles are "An Old Desk," "Among the Old Book-Stores," "How I Ran for the Presidency" (printed shortly before the 1872 election), and "How We Had Our Heads Examined." The old love for Irving, dating from that memorable afternoon in Virginia, and the fondness for Charles Lamb, almost as old in his memory, found an outlet in these *Hearth and Home* essays. Free to do what he liked with the magazine as long as he turned a profit for the owners, he wrote the fiction that commands our chief interest and, for his own and his readers' enjoyment, these essays that are readily dismissed as anachronisms or aberrations in the age of realism.

The reason Eggleston could relax with essays was the sudden astonishing success of his second serialized story, *The Hoosier School-Master*. All his earlier fiction had been of his own devising, but this time he had the advantage of daily contact with his brother George, who was a fluent talker grateful for the chance to report his varied adventures to the man he sometimes called his twin. One unforgettable experience was his having taught in a one-room rural school at Riker's Ridge, an Indiana crossroads community where Edward had once preached, and one much like the district the family had visited in the summer of 1850. "Uncle Sim's Boy" had been reasonably successful; Edward decided to turn George's reminiscences into another story of three installments. But the reader response was so insistent that he could not stop with three parts; he had to keep going for a total of fourteen weeks (September 30 to December 30) with little chance to plan ahead. The weakness of structure has been a general complaint, then and ever since, among the critics; the astonishing fact is that, under the conditions of composition, the book has any structure at all. Certainly uncritical readers were unconcerned; all that mattered to them was that Eggleston had succeeded, brilliantly, in producing a book-length story unlike anything ever written before and one that caught the popular fancy as few other American novels have ever done. He did not, like Byron, wake one morning to overnight fame; it is rather a matter of a rapid crescendo of fame, week by week, as the installments followed one another. But at the year's end Eggleston enjoyed a degree of fame he could hardly have imagined just three months earlier. It was his fondest boyhood dream come true.

## CHAPTER 4

# Realist at Work

## I  *Sudden Fame*

IN THE CONTEXT of a lifelong ambition to be an author, the publication of *The Hoosier School-Master* on December 15, 1871,¹ is the point that divides becoming from being. If at that moment Eggleston had stopped writing altogether, his fame would be hardly less secure than it is now; for it rests, perhaps too much, on this one book. Some writers never do achieve even this degree of recognition for books that are demonstrably much better. The importance of *The Hoosier School-Master* lies not in its artistic value but in its historical significance as the pioneer of western dialect novels; even if it were more lacking in artistry than it is, it would retain this importance and keep its author's name alive.

In fact, Eggleston lived to rue the vast popularity of that first book which led people to overlook his later, and better, books. The reputation of *The Hoosier School-Master* works also to the disadvantage of modern readers who, noting its obvious flaws, decide not to try the other novels, thereby denying themselves the pleasant discovery that *The Circuit Rider* and *Roxy* are well worth the time it takes to read them.

Reminiscing in 1890, Eggleston said of the process of writing *The Hoosier School-Master*, "I was only drawing on the resources which the very peculiar circumstances of my life had put at my disposal."² He also recalled, then and on other occasions, that Taine's *Philosophy of Art in the Netherlands*, which he reviewed in *The Independent* in 1870,³ had encouraged him to attempt the realistic portrayal of commonplace materials. Literary historians, in their laudable quest for lines of influence, have gratefully followed his lead in giving Taine a major share of the credit. A little second thinking, however, produces the suggestion that not even so eminent an authority as Taine could supply the original idea of writing about humble people in humble settings. It is more reasonable to say that Taine renewed and underscored a tendency already present—just as Lowell's practice and personal encouragement confirmed a long-standing impulse to record regional dialect. As for the "very peculiar circumstances" of his life, while they cannot be dismissed, it is evident that Eggleston used them more for general background than for plots or characters; indeed, he was often least effective when following fact most closely, as in *The Mystery of Metropolisville.* His negligible formal education has further misled historians into considering him an untutored "original" who created more from natural impulse than from conscious art. If anything, he was too bookish, too ready to be guided by what he had read. A greater freedom, a firmer reliance on impulse, would have strengthened his eventual reputation as a realist. His early preoccupation with religion and his years as a preacher also influenced his writing; not until he wrote *Roxy* did he let loose the moralistic brakes, and with laudable results.

*The Hoosier School-Master,* as noted earlier, began as a three-installment story and was extended in response to reader interest. The hero, Ralph Hartsock, is a not too muscular young teacher exposed, for the first time in his life, to the crudities of Flat Creek, a frontier community—George Cary Eggleston's actual experience at Riker's Ridge. The conflict is elemental: the agent of social advance (through education) is pitted against the retrogressive forces of ignorance, animal mischief, and malice—not to mention a deliberate effort to make him marry a local slattern. His first contact is with a most unfriendly bulldog; his second, with Jack Means, the leading school trustee, is hardly more reassuring: "It takes a *man* to boss this deestrick. Howsumdever, ef you think you kin trust your hide in Flat Crick school-house I ha'n't got no 'bjection. . . . They a'n't been no other applications. The last master had a black eye for a month."

Ralph never suffers a black eye, but he is put to a series of harrowing tests, any one of which would have justified his quitting. The bulldog of the opening scene provides him with a useful symbol: he too will be a bulldog, holding on grimly no matter what. The struggle for mastery in the schoolroom is eased when the school bully, Bud Means, out of some dim impulse to better himself, responds to Ralph's suggestion that the two of them comprise a "Church of the Best Licks." Bud helps clear him of a burglary charge in the climactic courtroom scene, although the turning point comes when a key witness, recently exposed to the hellfire-and-brimstone preaching of "Brother Sodom," blurts out the truth he had intended to hide.

In extending the narrative, Eggleston soon exhausted his brother's reminiscences and had to turn elsewhere, chiefly to familiar themes in other books and to his own memories of the Indiana hinterland. The latter provided the book's most vivid character, Dr. Smalley, who is only slightly altered from the Dr. Small who had been thought to be the most respectable citizen of Decatur County and whose exposure as a gang leader had been such a shock to Edward. When Eggleston turned to other fictional themes, however, the result was often melodrama. In this first book and in its successors, mysterious night-riding is so common that Alexander Cowie, one of the most sympathetic modern critics of Eggleston's fiction, has suggested an affinity with "the penny dreadfuls" of the period; Eggleston, he remarks, "often helped himself to stereotyped Gothic night scenes involving desperadoes."[4] Ralph is not the only Eggleston hero in danger of being hanged who is rescued melodramatically. The combination of just this element and the novelty of the setting and dialect most easily accounts for the enduring popularity of *The Hoosier School-Master* among common readers who favor it above more artistic achievement by followers whom its success encouraged.[5] But uncritical readers also liked the happy ending; in almost all Eggleston's novels the virtuous are rewarded and the villains are either converted or discomfited.

Eggleston changed Small's name to Smalley, but he was less discreet in using certain other names. It did not occur to him that a local paper in Vevay would reprint the story (without permission); he certainly had no intention of embarrassing his former neighbors. The only one of them who took offense publicly was Jeems Phillips, the champion speller; but it was easy to mollify him by reminding him that he *was* the champion in the book, as in life.

A more serious offense in the eyes of some cultured Indianians —and one that even today has not been entirely forgiven—was the impression of state backwardness that the book, overloaded as it is with crude and illiterate characters, could not help conveying, just as *God's Little Acre* and *Tobacco Road* have more recently confirmed an unfair image of the entire state of Georgia. Eggleston was aware of the possibility; his preface, dated "Brooklyn, December, 1871," contains this sentence: "I had some anxiety lest western readers should take offence at my selecting what must always seem an exceptional phase of life to those who have grown up in the more refined regions of the West." Readers *ought* to read prefaces, but they seldom do; and the novel does picture a society of caricatures—the Means tribe in all their meanness, the illiterate, hardshell preacher, the bound girl (Hannah, the heroine) kept in servitude by a falsified record of her age, and the preposterous Squire Hawkins with his glass eye, false teeth, dirty wig, swallow-tail coat, black gloves, and dyed whiskers.

Western readers might also have read in the preface Eggleston's hope of breaking the New England monopoly: "It used to be a matter of no little jealousy with us . . . that the manners, customs, thoughts, and feelings of New England country people filled so large a place in books, while our life, not less interesting, not less romantic, and certainly not less filled with humorous and grotesque material, had no place in literature. It was as though we were shut out of good society." Sensitive Indiana readers might further have observed that one of the most amusing portraits in this novel is that of Martha Hawkins, the squire's niece who has recently arrived from Massachusetts, bringing a wardrobe of linguistic absurdities capped by her favorite expression, "When I was to Bosting."

The conditions of composition make *The Hoosier School-Master* an inadequate example of Eggleston's method. What he did later, when he deliberately projected full-length books and gave time to their development, is more susceptible of evaluation. Understandably enough, part of what he did later was to use many of the same materials that had made the first book popular. Common to all, except *The Faith Doctor*, is the dialect, which he handled with the care of an expert and which gives his fiction a value for linguistic history. The spelling-bee in the *School-Master*, so well liked that it precipitated a national revival of "spell-downs," was not repeated, being replaced by other familiar customs of the frontier. *The Circuit Rider* opens with a corn-shucking; *The Graysons*, with "turning the Bible";

*Roxy,* with a barbecue, soon followed by a country hoe-down; and *The End of the World* ends with a "shiveree."

Eggleston's characters are too often stereotypes or caricatures, or they are eccentrics like Whiskey Jim, met earlier in "The Gunpowder Plot," who reappears in the first chapter of *The Mystery of Metropolisville;* or "the Inhabitant" of the same book; or the Backwoods Philosopher in *The End of the World.* Sometimes, however, such characters are considerably more interesting than the "normal" individuals; Plausaby, in *Metropolisville,* is a fascinating rogue, able to sell corner lots to the most hardened skeptic. He is possibly the best satirical portrait ever drawn of the skillful but unscrupulous real-estate promoter. The reverse technique of underplaying character is seldom found, but it is used with conspicuous success in *The Graysons,* in which the defense attorney is a young lawyer named Abraham Lincoln.

Conversely, in planning his subsequent novels Eggleston abandoned the domestic urban scenes of such stories as "Huldah the Help," "The Story of a Valentine," and "Uncle Sim's Boy." Only in his final novel, *The Faith Doctor* (1891), did he venture a city setting, although one unfinished work, *Agnostic,* is also urban; both turn on sophisticated metropolitan religious life.

*The Hoosier School-Master* is the one Eggleston novel that has enjoyed perennial popularity. In the period of nearly a century since its first appearance it has almost never been out of print, and readers have usually had the choice of more than one edition. Of all the many printings the most important is the Library Edition of 1892, for three reasons: it is the only edition for which Eggleston made needed revision, thus producing a final or "authorized" text; it has footnotes in which he explained many of the dialect terms; and it has a preface of twenty-odd pages in which he reviewed the book's history.

The textual revisions in the Library Edition are minimal because Eggleston, after twenty-one years, felt almost as if the book were somebody else's. "The author of 'The Hoosier School-Master' is distinctly not I," he wrote; "I am his heir and executor; and since he is a more popular writer than I, why should I meddle with his work?" The context of this rather peculiar remark is the grudge he bore the reading public for consistently indentifying him with this first novel and ignoring his later work.

The footnotes, concentrated in the early chapters, are valuable explanations of such terms as *aout, durn't, ketch, dog-on, plunder, 'low, chunk, peart, right smart, brash,* and *juberous.* Several of these terms appear also on the list of Hoosierisms that he jotted down in 1863; he may well have had the list at his elbow in both 1871, when he wrote the novel, and in 1892, when he added the notes. By the latter year he could approve, on scholarly grounds, his own prior use of dialect; his development as a methodical dialectician during the 1880's confirmed the acuity of his aural observation and the accuracy of his memory almost thirty years after his first exposure to Hoosier speakers. The point can hardly be overemphasized, for the dialect is the one element of the book's early popularity that has survived all changes in literary standards and all critical deprecation.

Among the manuscripts that Eggleston left unpublished is part of a lecture that he gave on numerous occasions, "The Hoosiers and the Hoosier Language." The second of the two surviving paragraphs shows something of his detailed acquaintance with Hoosierisms and also, in the final sentence, his sense of the importance of preserving it:

> The term Hoosier in its strictest application means a native of Indiana, but the Hoosier people proper, Hoosier by language and customs, comprise a large part of the inhabitants of Ohio, Kentucky, and that part of Illinois called Egypt on account of the abundance of corn and the darkness that can be felt. Peculiarities are not as prominent. In fact a man might travel thro' Indiana & know little of the pure Hoosier. It is in the back counties, off the lines of travel, in what are called hoop-pole counties in the "pocket," as the S. W. corner is called, that the Hoosier grows to perfection. . . . [The settlers] did not bring a large stock of erudition with them, and you would infer from quite a slight acquaintance with them that the school teacher was not much "abroad in the land." But the ever extending railroad lines and the present excellent school system are all serving to introduce the English language & to reduce the Hoosierishness of the Hoosier, and we must hasten if we are to succeed in photographing him before he fades from sight.[6]

Another unpublished fragment, sharply critical of an 1884 article by a college professor on "Negro Speech,"[7] is further evidence that Eggleston's early fascination with dialect was bolstered and refined by his historical research. Not until 1894, however, did he publish anything on the subject: "Wild Flowers of English Speech" and "Folk-Speech in America."[8] Eggleston alone of the pioneer realists became a student of dialect—probably because he turned to the writing of history. In 1871 he could not have written the explanations of the dialect he used in *The Hoosier School-Master;* when he could, in 1892, he only said what students of American dialect have amply endorsed since: that the dialect in that book is a distinctive and accurate contribution to linguistic history.

## II  *Exploiting a Genre*

The second novel, *The End of the World,* appeared soon after the first; its serial run in *Hearth and Home* extended from April 20 to September 7, 1872, and the book appeared immediately afterward. For his plot Eggleston went back to the Millerite delusion of the early 1840's; the climax, logically enough, comes on the precise night—in the novel, August 11, 1843—when the followers of William Miller, who are now called Second Adventists, gathered on hills to await the arrival of Jesus in person and the attendant destruction of the earth. Since Eggleston was only five years old in 1843, it is improper to suppose that this novel came out of his own experience; only the setting and the regional manners he carefully works in did.

Eggleston, who subtitled this novel *A Love Story,* set out to show young love triumphant over great difficulties. Julia Anderson has to contend with a jealous, vindictive shrew of a mother (Abigail) whose behavior approaches paranoia, and with a spineless father (Samuel) who submits meekly to endless henpecking. Abigail's violent opposition to Gus Wehle as a possible husband for Julia reflects a regional bias against all "Dutchmen"; the prejudice is shared by a number of the local youths who, led by Julia's worthless brother Norman, attempt to lynch Gus's father Gottlieb.

A slick mustachioed singing-master named Humphreys arrives in the rural community, takes lodging with the Andersons, and seeks methodically to win Julia. He discredits Gus, who is dismissed as the Andersons' hired hand and, shortly afterward, is branded as a thief and forced to flee. His replacement is Jonas Harrison, garrulous, amiable, and shrewd—one of Eggleston's most successful characters. In addition to wooing the hired girl

Cynthy Ann ("a good, pious, simple-hearted, Methodist old maid," to whom "everything pleasant had a flavor of sinfulness"), Jonas becomes an able ally of Julia's hermit-philosopher Uncle Andrew in helping Gus and in foiling both Humphreys and Mrs. Anderson.

Religious differences affect the developing action. Gus has been raised a Moravian, but his father is one of the early converts to Millerism. Cynthy Ann is dubious of the Free Light convictions of Jonas until a sensible presiding elder overrules the narrow judgments of two lesser Methodist clergymen. Humphreys adds to his other assorted villainies a glib pretense at orthodoxy, and he joins the Millerites when joining them becomes the fashion. Sam Anderson joins from conviction; he sells his farm for a mere fifty dollars, but not to Humphreys.

On the night of August 11, 1843, the devout, who have sold or given away the worldly possessions that they believe they will have no further use for, gather on a bald hill. Around them are the disbelievers, who burlesque their Millerite hymns and oratory. Uncle Andrew drily observes that it cannot be midnight everywhere on earth at the same moment, while Jonas casts cynical aspersions on Millerite arithmetic. A sudden thunderstorm with strong wind scatters the crowd; credulous and scoffer alike obey the impulse of self-preservation.

Earlier, aboard the riverboat *Iatan,* Gus discovers that Humphreys has another profession, gambling, and another name, Parkins. He fleeces Norman Anderson of almost a thousand dollars that he has collected for a business firm. Gus recovers the money for Andrew by threatening Humphreys with exposure at Paducah, where the local gentry are intent on vengeance. As reward for his trouble, he is dismissed from his post as striker (apprentice engineer) because the captain gets a share of the gambler's winnings. He barely manages to reach Uncle Andrew's bottomland "castle" before he collapses in a serious illness. Julia evades her mother's close surveillance to visit Gus, and she renews his wish to live.

On the night set for the earth's dissolution, the presiding elder marries Jonas and Cynthy Ann and then, using a license that Uncle Andrew has had the foresight to secure, Gus and Julia. Andrew reveals that it is he, acting through an agent, who has bought the Anderson farm; he also reveals that Abigail, after jilting him, contrived to exclude him from his rightful share in the property. But Andrew is generous; he gives Samuel half the farm and deeds the remainder to Gus and Julia. Despite these complications Eggleston manages an ending happy for almost everybody, even the discomfited Abigail; she is reconciled and softened. A letter from one of Gus's old friends on the *Iatan*, meanwhile, reports Paducah's revenge on the villainous Humphreys.

Uncle Andrew's bookishness gave Eggleston several opportunities to comment on literature. One volume in the castle library is Longstreet's *Georgia Scenes* (1835), which is today considered a classic of Southwest humor. On a single page Eggleston alludes to *Plutarch's Lives, The Merchant of Venice*, and Milton's conception of Hell. In the final chapter he mentions the New England limitations of Noah Webster's dictionary, which fails to list the term "shivaree." Such references are few, however, and hardly more intrusive than the fine old Methodist hymns that the presiding elder, after serving as a minor *deus ex machina*, sings lustily as he rides off to his next appointment.

*The Hoosier School-Master* had caught the reviewing fraternity off guard; none of the critics recognized it as a pioneering work. They were kindlier toward *The End of the World*, which later critics have viewed with slight enthusiasm; Cowie gives it very short treatment, and other historians tend to ignore it altogether. *Scribner's Magazine* had the most unusual review: it interpreted the *end* of the world—meaning its purpose—as "to love and be loved," and it found this end amply developed in the novel.[9] The contemporary welcome meant, for Eggleston, the assurance that he could live by writing novels and, more immediately, that he could withdraw from his editorial post on *Hearth and Home*. He received no royalties from *The Hoosier School-Master* until the Library Edition of 1892, and the attendant loss of income was a constant reminder to make favorable royalty arrangements for all his later books. With the income from each new novel he could support his family while he wrote the next. This statement is not entirely accurate, however; a major source of income during the early 1870's was his Sunday school books—theology, as it were, subsidized his fiction.

*The Mystery of Metropolisville*, the third novel, displeased most of the critics. It can still irritate readers, for it fails to introduce the mystery promised in the title until the two-thirds mark—to be precise, page 214 in a volume of 320 pages. In the process of composition even Eggleston became conscious of the mounting delay; on page 124 appears an author's aside of the sort that mar all his early novels:

> I fear the gentle reader, how much more the savage one, will accuse me of having beguiled him with false pretenses. Here I have written XIV chapters of this story, which claims to be a mystery, and there stand the letters XV at the head of this chapter and I have not got to the mystery yet, and my friend Miss Cormorant, who devours her dozen novels a week for steady diet, and perhaps makes it a baker's dozen at this season of the year, and who loves nothing so well as to be mystified by labyrinthine plots and counterplots—Miss Cormorant is about to part company with me at this point. She doesn't like this plain sailing. Now, I will be honest with you, Miss Cormorant, all the more that I don't care if you do quit. I will tell you plainly that to my mind the mystery lies yet several chapters in advance.

And so on for another half page.

Shortly afterwards, at the opening of Chapter XVIII, Eggleston remarks, "If this were a History of Metropolisville—but it isn't, and that is enough." At just this point he might have served his cause well by changing the title, from the *Mystery* to the *History of Metropolisville,* or even to the *Story,* which Edgar Watson Howe chose to do ten years later for *The Story of a Country Town,* a somewhat comparable novel. The specific mystery—who robbed the mail?—is actually too slight to sustain a novel of this length. It fits in readily enough when it finally is reached, but changing the book's title would not have required any change in the final episode.

"Words Beforehand" and "Words Afterward" make the explicit point that this is a story of a frontier community of brief existence, conceived in vapid dreams of quick enrichment but depending for survival on trickery and deceit instead of integrity and succumbing in the competition with stronger neighbors. The Minnesota counterpart of Metropolisville is Cannon City, the boom town where Eggleston spent most of his first short visit to the Territory; but it might have been any of the thousands of ghost towns that dot the nation's map today.

When the story opens, Albert Charlton is arriving on his first visit to Minnesota to join his mother and sister Katy, after

quitting college without a degree. Sharing his stagecoach from
Red Owl Landing are Mr. Minorkey, a money lender (at a
modest three to five per cent a month), and his handsome
daughter Helen. The driver is Whiskey Jim, or the "Superior
Being." Albert is quickly caught up in the chaotic life of the
new town. He becomes postmaster. He despises his stepfather,
Plausaby, whose suave skill in selling corner lots makes him the
key figure in the town's spurious progress.

"You are an Episcopalian, I believe?" said Plausaby, Esq.
The fat gentleman replied that he was a Baptist.
"Oh! well, I might have known it from your cordial way of
talking. Baptist myself, in principle. In principle, at least. Not
a member of any church, sorry to say. My mother and my first
wife were both Baptists. Both of them. I have a very warm
side for the good old Baptist church. Very warm side. And a
warm side for every Baptist. Every Baptist. To say nothing of the
feeling I have always had for you—well, well, let us not pass
compliments. Business is business in this country. In this
country, you know. But I will tell *you* one thing. The lot there
marked 'College' I am just about transferring to trustees for a
Baptist university. There are two or three parties, members of
Dr. Armitage's church in New York City, that are going to
give us a hundred thousand dollars endowment. A hundred
thousand dollars. Don't say anything about it. There are people
who—well, who would spoil the thing if they could. . . ."

The fat man's growing impatience overcomes Plausaby's reluctance to sell a lot intended for Katy Charlton—a device used
again and again—and the sale is made; Albert, intrigued by his
stepfather's glowing description of the lot, discovers that it is
at the bottom of a slough.

Albert finds much to do. Helen Minorkey is his one intellectual
peer; in spending every possible minute with her, he overlooks
Plausaby's niece and housekeeper, Isabel Marley. By tactless
condemnation of all doctors, lawyers, and clergymen, he wins
general hostility from the town's conventional citizens. He
assumes the role of his sister's protector against the wiles of
Smith Westcott, a compulsive talker, a purveyor of feeble jokes,
and an expert in minstrel show songs. He finds a stout ally in
George Gray, a shy Hoosier poet known as "The Inhabitant,"
who acts from a simple, tender, and hopeless affection for
Katy. Whiskey Jim is another loyal friend.

Were it not for the mystery in the final third of the book, the climax could have been the drowning scene, a vivid reworking of a tragic accident that Eggleston had witnessed in Cannon City. Westcott, barred from seeing Katy, works on her sympathy by threatening to throw himself into the lake. A girl of fifteen with an emotional maturity of about twelve, Katy has an abnormal fear, not so much of drowning itself as of being bled white, by leeches, "nasty, black worms—and one of them bit my hand once." A new sailboat, dangerously overloaded because Westcott ignores the helmsman's warning and insists on sitting beside Katy, overturns in a squall. Westcott starts ashore with Katy in tow but pushes her away when he fears she will pull him under. When her body is recovered by the Hoosier poet, her worst fears have been realized: she has been bled white by the leeches.

The way is now cleared for the mystery, which is introduced by means of a lurid news story in the *Wheat County Weakly Windmill*—a burlesque of small-town journalism. Albert is arrested for using a land warrant that had been mailed to Smith Westcott. Helen Minorkey at once washes her hands of him. He pleads innocent but refuses to say anything in his defense and is found guilty; he is sentenced to ten years in the Minnesota penitentiary at Stillwater. The local clergyman (an approximation of Eggleston himself in his Stillwater assignment), after becoming friendly with Albert, visits Metropolisville and secures a death-bed confession from his mother; Plausaby, it transpires, forced her to steal the warrant and give it to Albert as the gift of an anonymous friend. Discredited by the disclosure, Plausaby disappears; Eggleston reports that he "turned up afterward as president of a Nevada silver-mine company, which did a large business in stocks but a small one in dividends." His creditors make short work of his assets. Albert, pardoned, is suddenly a man of substance because some land he has pre-empted adjoins the surveyed route of a new railroad. He returns to Metropolisville and claims the long-deserving Isabel Marley; after a gay wedding dinner, he drives off with her to their new home in Charlton, a township which the Hoosier poet has named in memory of Katy.

This book is social history of a sort rarely captured in fiction because individuals living through a genuine frontier experience prefer to romanticize or, more often, to direct their literary impulses toward subjects less crude and stark. Reviewers were hardly interested in social history; and the starkness offended them. They also found fault with the crudeness of Eggleston's fictional structure, quite a different matter and, in all frankness, a fault more deserving of censure. He was distressed enough by the hostile reviews to consider abandoning fiction for a while; he changed his mind, but he was determined that next time would be different, as it proved to be.

Exactly why Eggleston could record convincingly the life of the Ohio Valley where he spent his first years, but not of the Minnesota frontier more recent in his experience, is a question not easy to answer. The magnified dimensions of that vast region, the open wheat country that stretches far north into Canada and westward across the Dakotas and Montana and down into Nebraska and Kansas, has a quality that eludes easy description. Terms suited to the third of a nation east of the Mississippi prove inadequate; the Vevay farm seemed very small when Eggleston saw it again after living a while in Minnesota. Human beings readily become masters of fields and pastures and meadows bounded by woodlots and hedgerows; the prairie country makes dwarfs of people. Not until the Norwegian Rölvaag wrote *Giants in the Earth* in 1927 did any author fully succeed in capturing the majesty of the region, the brooding emptiness, the silent threat to survival of a form of nature too vast to visualize. Others have succeeded since—A. B. Guthrie in *The Big Sky* and Wallace Stegner in *The Big Rock Candy Mountain*. One of the mysteries of *Metropolisville* is Eggleston's ability, as early as 1873, to do as well as he did in capturing the region's essence.

Cowie, who has lived in Minnesota, suggests in *The Rise of the American Novel* that the plot of Metropolisville is as inchoate as Minnesota was in its territorial period. The other Eggleston novels, it should be remembered, were set in parts of the Middle West that were settled and gained statehood much earlier—Ohio, Indiana, Illinois. Eastern reviewers showed little enough knowledge of these states; most of them were totally ignorant about Minnesota. Washington Gladden's review in *Scribner's*[10] is typical; it charges Eggleston with not knowing Minnesota, whereas it was obviously Gladden who was ignorant of it.

On June 16, 1873, Eggleston wrote to his daughter, "there seems to be a general conviction that I cannot plot. I believe that's about right. I am trying this time." It was a disadvantage to Eggleston that he never had a literary advisor, some writer of experience to point out flaws and to suggest techniques, as Hemingway had Gertrude Stein, and as Faulkner had Sherwood Anderson. His only critic-teachers were the reviewers, but he was wise enough to heed them—whenever they said anything worth heeding. The *Nation* never helped, for it characteristically balanced every statement with its opposite: the West was "not ill sketched," it had said of *The Hoosier School-Master*, but it was done "quite sketchily, to be sure." The story had "essential truth and some effectiveness," but "no interest of passion or mental power."[11] Its review of *Metropolisville* was no more satisfying: the setting was "not what it ought to be," and the book was "by no means the most entrancing story that was ever written. To a great many people it may present no interest whatsoever." The conclusion is a model of how not to leave a single positive impression: "still one would be inclined to say that without more care he will not rise above being what he is now, and that is the condition of a man who promises more than he has performed."[12]

But most reviews, whether hostile or friendly, provided some hint that a sensitive writer could follow to his profit. *Appleton's Journal*, for example, branded *The Mystery of Metropolisville* a very disagreeable book, with the strongest light thrown on the coarse characters and with caricatures introduced for the sake of introducing them, not to serve the plot.[13] The *Christian Union*, which liked the book and said it renewed the reader's faith in Eggleston's future, also criticized the introduction of eccentric characters who are subsequently forgotten.[14] Eggleston smarted under the *Appleton's* rebuke but saw that the *Christian Union* had made the same point—a fascination for odd characters without relating them convincingly to the other characters or to the action. He resolved in the future to avoid this fault and others noted in the reviews; he was particularly determined to write his next novel with great care.

The result was worth the self-discipline, for most of the reviews of *The Circuit Rider* were favorable, and so is the opinion of subsequent critics. The *Nation* cast doubt on its authenticity[15] and *Lippincott's* complained that the characters were insufficiently complex and individual,[16] but Howells in the *Atlantic* pronounced the book Eggleston's best to date,[17] while *Scribner's* called it the finest tribute ever paid to the preaching profession and to the pioneer Methodists of the Ohio Valley.[18] This last opinion was particularly gratifying, for Eggleston had meant the book to be just that. The dedication is to "my Comrades of Other Years, the brave and self-sacrificing men with whom I had the honor to be associated in a frontier ministry." It would have been humiliating for *The Circuit Rider* to be a failure, for he brought to its composition an unashamed devotion and sincerity that no other subject could have evoked. "I could not," he wrote in the preface, "treat the early religious life of the West otherwise than with the most cordial sympathy and admiration."

Yet he felt it necessary to alert his readers to the possibility that the story might be hard to accept: his preface opens with the striking sentence, "Whatever is incredible in this story is true." He went on to remark, with a certain grim pride, that he had "the right to celebrate" the hardships of the circuit "since they came so close to being the death of me." He could hardly have drawn so authentic a picture of circuit riders if he had not been one; yet it is wrong to assume that the novel is closely autobiographical. His chief boyhood heroes had been famous early preachers harassed by dangers of many kinds but contemptuous of life itself in their devotion to the cause. Such men, he never stopped believing, were the true heroes of the frontier, more important than Indian fighters. When in 1873 he planned his novel and set its time as just after 1800, it was logical to turn to the memoirs left by these men. A little notebook that he had begun to use while writing *The Mystery of Metropolisville* contains many details from Jacob Young's *Autobiography of a Pioneer* and scattered references to other noted circuit riders (though not to Peter Cartwright, now considered the most famous of them all). Close comparison of these notes to the finished novel shows clearly how derivative it is. The most conspicuous evidence is the conversion of Morton Goodwin, the hero, from a wild scofflaw to a Methodist preacher; this follows Jacob Young's actual experience.

Like the mystery in *Metropolisville*, Morton's conversion is deferred until fairly late in the novel; but instead of marring the development, the postponement gives Eggleston ample space to describe the crudeness and chaos of the frontier just after 1800. Morton's spiritual progression is a microcosm of the region's struggle toward civilized order; the region, like the individual, had to repudiate the impulse toward lawlessness and to find the means of controlling it. To such a man as Eggleston, aggressive organized religion was the principal agency of this control. But some churches proved to be better equipped than others for the heroic contest; and in that particular part of the frontier the best equipped was the Methodist, with its camp meetings and circuit riders, and with its deliberate exploitation of emotionalism.

At the outset, Morton is presented as an ordinary young man torn between good and bad impulses. The team he captains wins the corn-shucking contest which opens the novel, chiefly because his quiet confidence provides a better spur to victory than does the sneering bravado of the opposing captain. But Morton has his weaknesses. He would rather ride and hunt than attend church, but he sometimes endures the services just to please his pious mother. In his love of drinking and gambling, however, he never becomes an adept; he is the easy victim of a professional named Burchard, who becomes a sheriff only as a cloak for his night-riding, outlaw activities. The final step in Morton's downfall is being accused of stealing his own horse. He is saved from hanging only by the chance passing of a clergyman who recognizes him and vouches for him despite his knowledge that Morton, in the recent past, has joined with other youths in the mischievous heckling of church meetings. Remorse and an unquenched spark of integrity raise Morton from this low point into the Methodist ministry; he becomes a conscientious circuit rider.

Patty Lumsden, the girl Morton loves, undergoes a parallel conversion, from Episcopalian snobbishness to Methodist humility. She helps discredit her father, siding with her cousin Kike whom Captain Lumsden has sought to cheat in a land grab. Kike becomes a circuit rider but his physical frailty leads to his early death. The death-bed scene has a supernatural detail: a white dove flies into the room and alights on Kike's breast. A second supernatural element is introduced when two strange dogs accompany Patty on a dangerous night ride to warn Morton of a plot on his life. Another kind of danger that Morton escapes is marriage to Eliza Ann Meacham, the "praying girl." Burchard, who knows her past, threatens to expose Eliza if she persists in holding Morton to a promise of marriage that she insists he has made. The outlaw's change of heart begins when Patty nurses him back to health, and is completed when he reveals that he is Morton's long-lost brother. Morton, Patty, and Burchard are all thus satisfactorly reformed in character and purpose, and the novel ends with a definite victory for the forces of civilized order.

The plot, despite its elements of coincidence, melodrama, and the supernatural, shows a marked advance in Eggleston's fictional technique. No eccentric character is introduced and then forgotten; the only real eccentric is Mr. Brady, the schoolmaster, with his thick Irish brogue and quick wit; but he shares with all other characters a continuing, clear relationship to the developing action. Motivation is good. In short, *The Circuit Rider* is better proof than any of its three forerunners that Eggleston was capable of being a realist.

When he had not had good sources to follow in his earlier books and especially in *The Mystery of Metropolisville*, the result was disappointing. The deliberate effort to write more carefully than before had its own value, and so, no doubt, did the simple process of maturing. Care and maturity also had much to do with the success of his next novel, *Roxy*, which brought him to the peak of his artistic career. The final novels—*The Graysons* in 1888 and *The Faith Doctor* in 1891—show a falling off. As John Flanagan has wisely observed, "the later novels lack the gusto and animation of his early fiction."[19]

## III  *Fiction as Avocation*

The first four novels appeared with an almost clocklike regularity, nine months apart on the average. *Roxy,* which broke this pattern, was issued in 1878, four years later than *The Circuit Rider.* Howells had feared, and the *Nation* had condemned, the results of writing too fast; but the charge could never be made again. On Thanksgiving Day, 1873, Eggleston jotted down a few notes for a new book, but he abandoned it. He turned instead, the next year, to collecting the twenty-five pieces that comprise *The Schoolmaster's Stories, for Boys and Girls,* and to editing two elaborate subscription books, *Christ in Art* and *Christ in Literature.* But what counted more in deferring his next novel was his resumption of active preaching. Then, in 1880, he began an entirely new career as an historian. After 1874, he was never again a full-time writer of fiction but a man who occasionally wrote fiction as an avocation.

The Lee Avenue Congregational Church, in Brooklyn, invited Eggleston to its pulpit late in 1874; the church fathers believed he had the reputation and the dynamic personality needed to reverse the alarming decline in membership. They accepted his major conditions, that the church waive a formal creed and become non-denominational, and that his suggestion for a new name, "Church of the Christian Endeavor," be adopted. To emphasize the liberalism that he hoped to establish, he invited to preside at his inauguration the Reverend David Swing of Chicago, a preacher so radical that the Presbyterian Church had once put him on trial for heresy.

One other condition, private rather than theological, was an annual extended summer vacation. Eggleston had taken many trips on business; now, with a little more money, he was able to travel for pleasure. In the spring of 1873 he had visited his brother Joe in Virginia, finding a rare delight in the ash cake, the corn bread, and the dogwood.[20] That summer he discovered the Green Mountains; he climbed Ascutney and played croquet at Grafton, the "Paradise of Croquet."[21] The next summer he visited Quebec with Howells; his report, in the *Christian Union,* included the suggestion that Howells' *A Chance Acquaintance* was more helpful than any of the available guidebooks to the Province.[22] Compared to such excursions, his final trip to Minnesota in January, 1875, to preach and lecture was far less pleasant; time had reduced the number of people who knew him, and he felt like a stranger. The trip that meant the most was to Lake George in the summer of 1875; once the Egglestons had seen that region, they had no desire to explore farther for a summer home.

The *Phrenological Journal* described Eggleston in December, 1875,[23] as large in Mirthfulness, Causality, Constructiveness, and Benevolence, with a quick intuitive grasp, a rate of thinking that even his rapid speech could not keep up with, an impatience with fixed forms, and a tendency to overwork and breakdown. Apart from the jargon of this pseudo-science—and whether or not his thick crown of graying hair permitted exact measurements of his skull—the portrait was not inaccurate, even though it closed with a moralistic but entirely unnecessary warning that he should abjure luxury and strong drink. What such an analysis could not provide was any clue to the real man. His behavior is a better guide.

The Church of Christian Endeavor was not immune from attack; and, in defending it, Eggleston showed some of the qualities that the phrenologists had attributed to him. He particularly resented a published charge that he trimmed his discourse "to humor the money influence in his congregation."[24] In his second year as pastor he found it necessary to defend the men's Endeavor Club which he had organized, not as a sugar-pill method to gain members for the church but to provide good reading, recreation (including a shooting gallery), social intercourse, and mutual advice.[25] Non-denominationalism was bad enough, for the orthodox, without the addition of amusement; but Eggleston was by now far removed from orthodoxy. The Endeavor Club reached a membership of about a hundred. The Sunday school, meanwhile, soon numbered a thousand. The church, by whatever measurement, was a success at a time when non-sectarian churches were rare.

A request early in 1876 for a set of his published works to be displayed at the Centennial Exhibition drew a cool reply; the retail price would mean a total of $17.25, which seemed steep to him.[26] Books were property—a point he later belabored in working for improved international copyright. *Roxy,* slowly taking shape, was delayed not only by the demands of his church but also by his increasing concern for its artistic quality. He told Howells as early as June, 1875, that it was half finished.[27] Finally completed two years later, it was accepted by *Scribner's* just before Eggleston sailed for Europe, alone.

The old dream of seeing Europe was coming true, but the dream had not included the public demonstration his departure occasioned. A small steamboat, the *Fletcher,* was rented by the Endeavor Club for club and church members, literary and other friends, and members of his family. At the last moment Eggleston crossed by a gangplank to the *Devonia,* some of whose other passengers thought he must be a famous politician. The *Daily Times* report worked in a plug for *Roxy* and called Eggleston "one of the most graphic, pungent, keen-sighted, and ready-witted of American novelists."[28]

Except that Lizzie was not with him, this first visit to Europe was a satisfying fulfillment of an old hope. Like most other Americans spending their first summer abroad, he tried to see everything in a short time. He landed in Ireland and quickly toured the fashionable show-places—the chasm at Carrick-a-rede, the Giant's Causeway, the vice-regal palace at Dublin. He rode in a jaunting car, closely observed the peasant poverty, and talked with many people, especially priests. His impressions on this and another visit to Ireland were enough to form one of the most successful and widely presented lectures he ever gave. He opened with the first two stanzas of Father Prout's "The Bells of Shandon" and for well over an hour kept his audience at a peak of attention with his rapid, witty, vivid word pictures of Ireland and the Irish.[29]

From Ireland he crossed to Chester and was soon in London for a fortnight of sightseeing. A performance of *Pilgrim's Progress* by the family of George MacDonald, the pious Scottish novelist, was one of the highlights; later he visited the MacDonald home in Hammersmith, staying for both tea and supper and enjoying the occasion much more than a luncheon put on by the Routledges (prominent publishers sometimes accused of pirating of American authors' books), where wine seemed to be the main course.[30] Crossing to the Continent, he visited Paris, Versailles, Geneva, the Alps, and the lakes of northern Italy but with diminishing interest; his pace was tiring, and he was increasingly homesick for his family. He kept them well informed, writing long, detailed reports and impressions every second or third day. He also sent three articles that appeared in the Brooklyn *Daily Times*,[31] which helped pay for the trip.

In Paris, a lingering Puritanism kept him from attending the opera and the theatre. "Paris is not bad in the way that New York & London are bad," he remarked. "The French violate morals but they almost never violate good taste."[32] Geneva was spoiled for him because U. S. Grant, on the grand tour that followed his release from the White House, was also there; and his welcome was more exuberant than Eggleston deemed necessary, since it interfered with his sleep.[33] It was a relief to join a party of tourists climbing Montanvert and crossing the Mer de Glace, and to pronounce judgment on the Italian lakes—Como alone, he thought, equalled Lake George for beauty.[34]

But it was an even greater relief to come home again, to his family, to the "dear noble church," and to Lake George.

Lillie's marriage on November 21 to Elwin Seelye of Queens-
bury, a village near the lake, cemented the family's tie with that
section; two years later, with the building of the "Owl's Nest"
at Dunham's Bay, Lake George became Eggleston's one permanent address for the rest of his life.[35] It would have been
difficult to find a lovelier, more peaceful place to live.

*Roxy* was serialized in *Scribner's* from November, 1877, until
the following October. Having given it so much time and hard
writing, Eggleston watched its progress, month by month, with
the mounting anxiety of a father for his most carefully nurtured
child. Failure might justify the objections that Josiah Holland
had raised just before the European trip. Mrs. Holland and
Richard Watson Gilder, after reading the manuscript, had
agreed with Josiah that several changes were needed: Roxy
was too undignified as a heroine's name, Nancy Kirtley should
be radically altered, the local color should be reduced, and the
entire first quarter of the book needed rewriting. If Gilder
were allowed to edit the book, Holland suggested, his prudence
might balance Eggleston's boldness.[36] The weeks in Europe
served as a cooling-off period; when he returned, Eggleston
was able to override all these objections. The reception of *Roxy*
was a vindication: within a month of its appearance in book
form, a fourth printing of five thousand copies was announced—
a firmer rate of sale than for any of his other novels.[37]

In his notes for *The Circuit Rider* Eggleston had expressed
an impulse to deal frankly with sexual attraction but had decided
it would not do for such a magazine as the *Christian Union,*
where it was to appear first in serial form. *Scribner's Monthly,*
despite the excessive caution of Holland, Mrs. Holland, and
Gilder, was a more sophisticated magazine and it reached an
audience less likely to be offended by the theme of marital
infidelity. Some of the reviewers disliked the theme but praised
Eggleston's way of handling it in *Roxy.* Harriet W. Preston was
one of these; in her *Atlantic* review[38] she bracketed Eggleston
with George Eliot in the ability to picture vulgar people without
being vulgar himself. She was more distressed by the book's
length—it is the longest of Eggleston's novels.

The story, in essence, records the spiritual maturing of Roxy
Adams, daughter of a crotchety but generous shoemaker in
Lucerne, an Ohio River town strongly reminiscent of Vevay.
At the outset Roxy is too good to be true; in her Christian piety,

in her sacrificing herself for the poor and the ill of the village, and especially in her patient care of her half-wit cousin Bobo, she is virtually a saint. Her closest friend, mischievous Twonnet Lefaure, laughs at her and remarks, to others, that Roxy would like nothing better than martyrdom. It seems probable that Roxy will marry the Presbyterian minister, Whittaker, her equal in nobility of character and in literal application of ideal Christian ethics but considerably wiser and more reflective than she.

Whittaker is lacking, however, the masculine attractiveness of handsome Mark Bonamy, local candidate for the state legislature. In his campaign rounds with Tom Leathers, the candidate for sheriff, Mark alienates most of the voters of Rocky Fork, a poor white precinct, by giving his entire attention, at a hoedown, to the local beauty, Nancy Kirtley. In the election, Mark gets very few votes in Rocky Fork, as the astute Leathers has predicted; but he wins his seat and sets off, on horseback, for the session in Indianapolis.

Summoned home by the death of his mother, Mark attends a Methodist revival (which Whittaker deplores as too loosely emotional) and basks in the admiration he wins by taking a prominent part. When he secures a Methodist license to preach and announces his intention of going to Texas as a missionary, Roxy is suddenly interested in him. She rejects Whittaker and marries Mark. At their "infare," attended by most of the villagers, the unhappy Whittaker discovers he is not alone in his misery; Nancy, on the strength of some gifts from Mark, insists she still has a claim on him and vows to avenge herself.

Mark's father, Colonel Bonamy, a former Congressman, intimidates Nancy with a barrage of legalistic terms. He also intrigues to dissuade Mark from going to Texas, but succeeds, on the day scheduled for the departure, only by suffering a stroke; Mark is now forced to stay, and he gradually loses his religious fervor. Eggleston says of him, "He was not bad, this Mark Bonamy. He was only one of those men whose character has not hardened." An ecclesiastical rebuke for attending a circus further cools his fervor; it also gives Eggleston the opportunity to comment about puritanical tradition:

> Brave old ironside forefathers! Blessings on you for chopping Charles Stuart's head off, and planting Plymouth Rock! You freed us from the Middle Ages; for which thanks. But you straightway

bound upon us your own severe prejudices, and they have come down to us by all hands. The most dominant influence in this English-speaking world of ours to-day, is not that of Shakspere, but of the men who hated him and his play-house. The Puritan preachers, the brave cobblers and tinkers, whom the seventeenth century stuck in the stocks and prison-houses, and the fervent Wesleyan village blacksmiths and Yorkshire farmers of the eighteenth century are still masters of the nineteenth. To this day we take our most innocent amusements in a guilty and apologetic fashion, bowing to the venerable prejudice, and saying: "By your leave, sir."

Roxy, after about a year with Mark, discovers that instead of a missionary bound for Texas she has married a popular young lawyer. Her reaction to his relaxed behavior is to redouble her piety, and to such a degree that political colleagues warn Mark that she is becoming a handicap to his career. They quarrel. Soon afterwards, while electioneering in the rain, Mark seeks refuge in the Kirtley cabin—and stays for twenty-four hours. Roxy, one of the last to learn about his infidelity, leaves Mark's house and moves in with Twonnet.

Whittaker now takes the lead. He subdues Nancy's fierce desire for vengeance, diverts Mark's mind from suicidal thoughts, and brings Roxy to an awareness that she can and should help both Nancy and Mark. Seeing Mark's anguished face at her window is a further spur to Roxy. She goes to Nancy with a promise to adopt her unborn child; and then she returns to Mark. The effort produces physical collapse; for a week she raves in a fever, and comes so close to dying that Mark thinks she is dead and rushes away. But she recovers and waits, numbly, for Mark to come back. Nancy visits her, for one final glimpse of her child before leaving the region with Jim Mc-Gowen, an old Rocky Fork beau who has married her. Mark, working on a steamboat, learns that Roxy is still alive; and the reunion, presumably for good, ties the final loose ends of the plot. But one brief added episode is necessary: Roxy, in church alone the next Sunday, knows, for the first time in her life, the utter joy and peace of genuine religious feeling. Not through calculated good behavior, not even by self-sacrifice of the noblest sort, but only by suffering and forgiving, Eggleston implies, can a human being gain this feeling.

If this is the ultimate point that Eggleston wished to make, Miss Preston's criticism in the *Atlantic* was unjustified: she thought that what followed the reconciliation of saintly wife and sinning husband tended to destroy the book's artistic symmetry. The reviewer for the *Nation* was even wider from the mark, objecting to Roxy's saintliness without realizing that the author was trying to expose its shallowness. This reviewer also objected to Nancy's animal beauty as sensational and unreal and to the book in its entirety as an unlovely sketch of Ohio Valley life.[39] *Scribner's Magazine* was able to provide an objective review of a book it had just finished serializing—an example of the left hand not knowing what the right hand was doing. Its reviewer sensed a certain baldness of outline: "It is not euphemism that is lacking, but mellowness,—the sublimated treatment which in Hawthorne makes us content to dwell upon the disagreeable, even the morbid."[40] *Harper's* reviewer supposed that the sensuous descriptions, especially of women who were magnificent animals, would tickle the unregenerate palate.[41]

Miss Preston's comparison of Eggleston with George Eliot occurred to other reviewers too, especially to the anonymous critic of the British *Vanity Fair,* who placed the book between *Scenes of Clerical Life* and *Middlemarch* and described Roxy herself as "a Methodist Romola." All the characters were a welcome contrast to the sawdust figures of Dickens' *Martin Chuzzlewit;* the portrayal of Nancy Kirtley showed an insight that George Meredith might envy.[42] Eggleston was generally dubious about British opinions of American literature, but this review, one of the most favorable any book of his ever received, was extremely gratifying. It showed, for one thing, that when an American realist was truest to his own creative impulses and did not let himself be swayed by editors' objections or by the possible effect on readers, he could win an international applause denied to more self-conscious efforts to gain approval. In any event, *Roxy* proved unusually successful in Great Britain, in sales as well as in critical opinion. At home, meanwhile, authorities of Wellesley College banned the book as improper.[43]

A comparison of *Roxy* with *The Hoosier School-Master* shows how far Eggleston progressed in seven years. The election barbecue, the country hoedown, the revival, and other local customs bear an integral relation to the plot instead of resembling cardboard props. Caricature is minimized; the people in the story are well realized, and clearly differentiated, through their dialect and behavior, not only ethnically—poor whites, Negroes, old French settlers—but socially as well. When he made Mark Bonamy a lawyer and a member of the legislature, Eggleston must have recalled his father's career. He took his central incident from an actual event in the family of his beloved teacher, Mrs. Dumont, and he used the old Dumont house as the Bonamy residence. Remembered settings, customs, incidents, and personalities are properly transmuted into *fiction*. There is even a trace of symbolic parallels: Mark resembles Marc Antony, with Nancy as his Cleopatra; Roxy is a saint, and the Reverend Mr. Whittaker suggests Jonathan Edwards.[44]

All things considered, *Roxy* marks the high point in Eggleston's art. It was the first novel he took time enough to write. It was also the last novel he wrote before becoming primarily an historian. If, instead of turning to history, he had remained a novelist and if he had continued to improve, American fiction would almost certainly have been the beneficiary. But *Roxy* is a good enough book for Eggleston's case to rest on.

## IV  *Late Fiction*

Fiction was increasingly an avocation during the final twenty-two years; whatever hours or weeks Eggleston chose to devote to imaginative writing were at the expense of history. Aware as he was that history needed his undivided attention if he were to make any kind of mark as an historian, the publication of three novels and several short stories after 1880 can be attributed only to his lingering inability, or unwillingness, to hew without pause to any single mark.

The first of these late novels—and the sixth in his total list— was *The Hoosier School-Boy*, serialized in *St. Nicholas* from December, 1881, to April, 1882, and issued in book form early in 1883. It is so thin and anemic a story that it hardly deserves critical attention. Eggleston viewed it frankly as a pot-boiler, written to provide a little income while he was laboring over his initial historical essays. The sales were a pleasant surprise; by October, 1883, a second printing had boosted the number in print to six thousand. "If they sell 5000," he wrote to his wife, "I get $525—all I expect."[45]

One reason for the book's appeal, then and later, was no doubt the nostalgic pleasure it provided many of its older readers. Will D. Howe, in an introduction he wrote for a 1936 edition, recalled his own Indiana school days, later than Eggleston's but not greatly different: the same poorly heated single classroom, the same corporal punishment by stern schoolmasters, the same "lessons in arithmetic, geography, Webster's spelling book, and McGuffey's readers" that "had their value in being very definite and not confused with many subjects and perhaps a superficial treatment as sometimes happens today."[46]

Plot is almost invisible in *The Hoosier School-Boy*. Jack Dudley, a shy, frail newcomer of thirteen, has a difficult time winning acceptance at the school in Greenbank (which is one more fictional name, along with New Geneva and Lucerne, for Eggleston's native Vevay). Pewee Rose, the school bully, and his cowardly lieutenant Will Riley bar Jack from the usual recess game of "three-hole-cat." Jack is patient; he shows new games to the younger boys. On one occasion he makes a yarn ball, and Eggleston remarks: "I have described the manufacture of the old-fashioned home-made ball, because there are some boys, especially in the towns, who have lost the art of making yarn-balls." Elsewhere Eggleston writes, "I suppose there are boys who do not know what 'Anthony-over' is," and in a footnote he suggests an "une-deux-trois" etymology for "Anthony." Jack Dudley's adjustment, slender as it is as a story line, is thus often subordinated in the earlier parts of the book to the description of games that Eggleston lovingly recalled from his boyhood.

A counter theme is the tyranny of many of the older schoolmasters, here well represented by Mr. Ball, a virtual sadist. How a community can rid itself of such a man is treated at some length; he carefully avoids punishing the children of influential citizens, who thus have no direct reason for dismissing him. Ball makes his critical mistake in switching little Columbus Risdale, not realizing his relationship to Dr. Lanham. Retribution is swift; but, when he is forced into retirement, no other teacher is available, and the school shuts down. Susan Lanham conducts a class informally, while Jack and a chum attend a school just across the Ohio River in Kentucky. Kindly Judge Kane helps Jack recover half of the thousand dollars owed his mother by a cold-hearted speculator. Jack's foot-race to file the claim is the one climactic moment in the story.

When a new teacher is finally found, one who substitutes moral suasion for the birch switches, Jack is able to secure the schooling he knows he needs. He rescues a non-swimmer, gets cramps for his effort, and is carried home, unconscious, by schoolmates including his former tormentors; henceforth he is fully accepted by his peer group. In addition, he secures a job as night-clerk in a drugstore, the first step, by implication, toward an eventual career in medicine.

Two years after *The Hoosier School-Boy* was published, Eggleston had another reason to suspend his history: a break in his health, serious enough for his physician to advise foreign travel. As had happened before, total suspension of mental activity was welcome only briefly; he was soon ignoring Europe's scenery while he worked on the elaboration of a familiar Lincoln anecdote—the clearing of a murder suspect by timely reference to an almanac. By January, 1886, he had written fifteen thousand words and supposed he would need only another ten thousand. For a title he wavered between *Circumstantial Evidence* and *Some Illinois Folks, a Rustic Story,* but he settled finally on *The Graysons.* In one letter home he reported that it was very encouraging to find he could construct a story with characters in it more real than those in Henry James's *The Bostonians.*[47] The more he wrote, however, the more words he seemed to need.

When the manuscript was finished, the Century Company delayed its decision about whether to accept it; and then, after deciding favorably, it deferred its appearance so long that Eggleston was thoroughly exasperated. Its serial run in the *Century Magazine* began, finally, in November, 1887, and continued until the next August. When it appeared as a book it sold slowly, despite the inclusion of Lincoln. Eggleston blamed Roswell Smith's opposition to the large discounts demanded by book-jobbers. Whatever the reason, only two thousand copies were sold in the first four months.

In locating *The Graysons* in Illinois, for the purpose of introducing Lincoln as a little-known lawyer, Eggleston altered only slightly the setting of his Indiana novels. The Ohio River is missing, but Moscow is the familiar small-town county seat;

Broad Run is the equally familiar settlement of lawless poor whites, while the rural countryside dominates and dwarfs both communities.

Tom Grayson, living with an uncle in Moscow while he reads law, is persuaded by George Lockwood to play cards with ne'er-do-well Dave Sovine. He loses all his own money and some lent to him by Lockwood, whose chief interest is the hope of detecting Dave's method of cheating. The escapade is quickly broadcast by small-town gossip; Tom loses the support of his uncle and the company of Rachel Albaugh, the local beauty. Lockwood's sanctimonious advice, never to gamble again, so infuriates Tom that he says, and repeats before witnesses, that he'll shoot him if ever their paths cross again. Tom goes home to the farm, his dream of a law career ended.

Hard work proves a sedative, but Tom becomes increasingly moody and pessimistic. In the hope of seeing Rachel, he attends a camp meeting but leaves early when he finds she is not there. Later that evening George Lockwood is found dead, not far from the camp meeting; Dave Sovine reports that he saw Tom do the shooting. The sheriff takes Tom to jail. Jake Hogan, a Broad Run man with a grudge against Tom, leads several attempts to lynch him which Bob McCord, a giant of a man, manages to thwart. At the coroner's inquest, feeling against Tom runs so high that his friends have to spirit him away.

Lincoln, an old friend of the Grayson family, agrees to serve as defense attorney, without a fee. At the trial he is entirely passive, waiving cross-examination of witnesses to the puzzled distress of Tom's supporters. Hiram Mason, the schoolteacher who is in love with Tom's sister Barbara, finds the whole process unendurable; in describing his agony, Eggleston produced one of his best figurative passages: "The law had the aspect of a relentless boa-constrictor, slowly winding itself about Tom, while all these spectators, with merely a curious interest in the horrible, watched the process. The deadly creature had now to make but one more coil, and then, in its cruel and deliberate fashion, it would proceed to tighten its twists until the poor boy should be done to death."

Only when Dave Sovine takes the witness stand does Lincoln come to life. Dave swears that he could see Tom, pistol in hand, at a distance of twenty feet, in the moonlight. Lincoln badgers him, reducing him to a trembling hulk before drawing from his pocket a small almanac: the murder was known to have been committed between ten and eleven, but the almanac shows that the moon did not rise that night until one o'clock. Dave, already close to collapse, confesses to the crime. Later, while awaiting execution, he explains that Lockwood had finally learned how he cheated at cards.

The villain's exposure and punishment follow the usual Eggleston formula, and so does the engagement of Hiram and Barbara—the virtuous made happy. But when Rachel Albaugh virtually throws herself at Tom, who is now a hero, he rejects her and she marries another old friend instead. Tom even declines his uncle's offer of renewed help. It almost seems as though Eggleston, for once, balked at an ending of perfect fictional justice.

Before he began to write *The Graysons,* Eggleston had supposed he was through with western fiction. As early as 1873, in fact, during the serial run of *The Circuit Rider,* he made some notebook jottings for a novel with a metropolitan setting. He had by then been living in and near big cities for seven years, four of them in Chicago and Evanston, three in Brooklyn and New York. Rural and small-town life was receding from his immediate experience. "I think myself," he wrote in his notebook, "more at home among the bourgoisie [*sic*]." But the story, which he entitled *Thomas Good's Wife,* got no further than rough outlines of three characters. One of these, the hero, was modeled upon Eggleston's brother-in-law William Goodsmith; he was to be "disinterested but always explaining away his goodness. . . . It will," Eggleston supposed, "be a variation from all precedent to create such a hero."

Not until 1890, however, did Eggleston carry out his wish to write a metropolitan novel. The preface to *The Faith Doctor* opens on just this topic: "Though there is no life that I know more intimately and none that I have known for so long a period as that of New York, the present story is the first in which I have essayed to depict phases of the complex society of the metropolis."

He began the book just after Lizzie's death; concentration on the fortunes of his fictional creations, he found, was an antidote to the "ennui and qualms of the old heart-break."[48] As a plot nucleus he used an unpublished short story, "An Irregular Practitioner"; he had read it in manuscript three or four years earlier and now bought it outright from the author, Anne Steger Winston of Richmond.[49]

One character existed ready-made—Thomas Good. Eggleston lifted him from the notes made in 1873; gave him a name more suitable to his social status, Philip Gouverneur; and added such traits as a passion for rare books in fine bindings. Other characters yield the impression that Eggleston modified individuals he had known or observed in New York. The fashionable Bible-reader Mrs. Frankland, however, bears a certain resemblance to Miss Birdseye in *The Bostonians*, the James novel that Eggleston had disliked in 1886. Phillida, the heroine, on the other hand, has some of Eggleston's own qualities, as does the Reverend Mr. Lurton in *The Mystery of Metropolisville*.

Differences among the Western novels become trivial compared with the very wide gulf that separates all of them from *The Faith Doctor*. This book belongs in the genre that includes *Washington Square* by Henry James, *A Hazard of New Fortunes* by Howells, and *Esther* by Henry Adams—novels of society in New York. Eggleston's remark in his preface to the Library Edition of *The Hoosier School-Master*, that after twenty-one years it seemed to be the work of another man, might just as well have been said about *The Graysons*, only three years older than *The Faith Doctor*. Certain structural devices that kept recurring as long as he wrote about the West, and that constitute his trade-mark as a Western realist, are conspicuously absent in this final novel. Author asides are almost nonexistent, and so are dialectal crudities; unwittingly, in 1891 Eggleston left dialect for Stephen Crane to exploit in *Maggie*. Gothic elements— night rides, disguised villains, and the supernatural—do not appear. The opposing parties are all civilized beings, separated from the rough and the crude by a substantial urban buffer.

The two principals, Charley Millard and Phillida Callender, are distinct New York types. Charley is the archetypal small-town boy (from upstate New York) who moves to the big city to make good, and succeeds. He is no penniless Horatio Alger hero, however, for an uncle has left him a tidy nest-egg of about seventy-five thousand dollars. Since part of this money is in stock of the Bank of Manhadoes, he has little difficulty securing a good position in that bank. Affable, considerate, discreet, and ambitious, he quickly adopts the manners approved for acceptance by good society. A few social *gaffes* (like wearing the wrong tie at a formal dinner) serve only to spur him on to total propriety. He can never hope to gain the absolute security of his friend Philip Gouverneur, who can laugh at pretensions and say that "the further away your forefather is, the more the virtue. Ancestry is like homeopathic medicine, the oftener it is diluted the greater the potency." Charley discovers and with studied off-handedness exploits some important ancestors to impress those who judge him; among these is Philip's mother, who disapproves of Astors and Vanderbilts and families of even more recent wealth.

Charley is loyal to his aunt, Mrs. Martin, who lives on Avenue C in Mackerelville, a very unfashionable section of New York. It reassures him to learn that even the oldest and wealthiest families also have poor relations. Philip's cousin Phillida Callender is one of these. Charley and Phillida become engaged. As saintly as Roxy, Phillida discovers that she possesses the power to cure certain physical conditions by faith and prayer. Her own moral strength has a contagious quality; almost by hypnotic inspiration she rids one child of the St. Vitus' Dance and helps Mina Schulenberg to rise from her wheel chair and walk. The Bible-reader Mrs. Frankland encourages Phillida, even to the point of standing firm against Millard, who is horrified by the increasing notoriety that the cures have stimulated among the members of his club. Standing firm has the undesirable effect, however, of a broken engagement.

Phillida is not such a zealot that she can forget Charley by intensifying her faith-doctor efforts. Instead, she almost at once realizes her delusion. Mina contracts a disease not susceptible to mental suggestion and dies, even after treatment by a neighborhood doctor. A Christian Science practitioner, Miss Bowyer, insists that faith healing is primitive and offers to make Phillida a partner. When Mr. Martin calls Miss Bowyer in to cure his son's diphtheria, Phillida swallows her pride and appeals to Charley for help. With the proper medical care that Charley secures, the boy recovers; but Phillida herself becomes desperately ill. A strong sense of failure and of blighting the happiness of others, Charley among them, prolongs her illness; she wishes to die. Only by disregarding the conventions that he almost worships can Charley renew her interest in living.

Philip Gouverneur, in love with Phillida himself and jealous of Charley's success with her, proves his essential nobility by sacrificing his hopes to their happiness. After the reconciliation, he says to Phillida, "I wanted to be able to think of you and Charley happy together without calling myself bad names, you know." To this Phillida replies, "I know. You never did a generous thing in your life without explaining it away." On their honeymoon the Millards send Philip, from London, a rare edition that he has long wanted.

The late recrudescence of the literary impulse did not burn itself out in the writing of *The Faith Doctor*. On Christmas Day, 1891, starting with a plot suggested by Lillie, Eggleston began the most extensive set of notes he ever wrote for any novel. The first of these notes were actually written down, at his dictation, by his second wife Frances, whom he had married barely a month before. This was the first instance of the extensive literary aid she provided in the remaining years of his life. The tentative title, *Agnostic*, suggests the central theme the book would have had; it also reflects Eggleston's own final position in theology, the complete opposite of his original orthodox piety.

*Agnostic* was to be another novel of New York society. The notes show the same preoccupation with individuals at different social levels, and the same overly detailed concern with specific streets, squares, and sections. After attending a lecture by Major Bowen of the Salvation Army, Eggleston carefully recorded her remarks about uplift work in the city's tenements and brothels. On some of his afternoon strolls he noticed, and later noted down, such things as a junk dealer's quarters, a stonecutter's blocks of rough-cut stone, boys playing at street games, ice-cream vendors, and an undertaker's window displaying a child's white coffin. The grist for his creative mill was no longer actuality recalled from the past and from distant places but the actuality of the immediate present, observed on the spot.

During the first weeks of shock after Lizzie's death, Eggleston had found a strange solace in reading the short stories of De Maupassant. At one time his religious scruples would have forbidden such reading, and even when he was further along on his road to religious heterodoxy, he read such authors with strong disapproval. Now, however, in search for ideas for the new novel, he turned to another French realist: "Note how Flaubert makes his characters 'flesh and blood' as in dwelling on the physical development of Charles Bovary." He determined to make bodily presence palpable, by means of small physical details, before introducing any more subjective considerations. "The last thing one gets acquainted with," he noted somewhat ruefully, "is the interior of a man." This recognition of the possibilities of character portrayal came too late to have any effect on his fiction, for *Agnostic* was never finished; but it is interesting that even Eggleston felt the influence of the European naturalists that is viewed as a major part of the redirection of American writing in the 1890's.

From the tone of the final notes, *Agnostic* would have carried sexual frankness much further than Eggleston had dared to do in *Roxy*. In that earlier book, the reader is told that Mark Bonamy sought refuge from the rain in Nancy Kirtley's cabin and stayed a whole day. In *Agnostic*, however, a scene that Eggleston labeled the "insurrection of the flesh" gives the details of a meeting between Giles and Genevieve in which the woman virtually asks to be a partner in adultery. "She discloses her feelings in spite of herself by stammering and inconsequential talk about her friendship for him and the hardships of her married life. . . . She disavows with horror any thought of going away. Is indignant, trembles, says indifferent things but again reveals the depth of her passion." Giles, not quite so far gone in his infatuation, is caught off guard. "Blindly in self-defense Giles closes the interview. Seeks relief in thought. Vain. Then in work." And as Eggleston wrote on a different page, "What man so nice or good as never to have had this fiend at his gate?" The sexual impulse may differ with time; in more civilized ages "The vile beast is only tamer."

Eggleston was fifty-four years old when he outlined *Agnostic*. The great change in American fiction, toward much greater frankness and the inclusion of naturalistic concepts, was to be the work of younger men—Stephen Crane, Frank Norris, Harold Frederic. Had he been a little younger, and not so strongly committed to the writing of social history, the completion and publication of *Agnostic* would have put him in the forefront of the new writers; it would also have confirmed his own opinion that the Eggleston of the 1890's was indeed a stranger from the author of *The Hoosier School-Master*.

## CHAPTER 5

# Social Historian

## I  *Transition*

CHANGES in the course of his life were, by 1880, an old story with Eggleston—in and out of the ministry in Minnesota, from preaching to journalism in 1866, to novel-writing in 1871, and back into the pulpit in 1874, to mention only the major turnings. In addition were the numerous sporadic ventures that add dashes of color to the total picture but mar its clarity. The early alternation of ambitions, religious and literary, formed a habit too strong for him to break in his maturity; even after committing himself to the writing of American history, he was easily distracted by other interests. What may be the most astonishing fact of his life is the readiness with which he launched out on a new career he had no training for and that he did so shortly after achieving in *Roxy* a novel that showed promise of significant, further growth in fiction. On first glance, this final major decision may seem a crowning example of erratic behavior.

The new shift in direction was not, however, as sudden and quixotic as it might appear. It did not remove him from the "life of the intellect" which he had yearned for as a boy when he was not yearning for greater piety—far from it; writing history requires a much more rigorous intellectual discipline than writing fiction. In his reading, Eggleston had always been attracted to history. Among the hundred-odd books that he owned in 1858 when at Traverse des Sioux were such classics as Rollin's *Ancient History*, *Plutarch's Lives*, Josephus' *History of the Wars of the Jews*, D'Aubigné's *History of the Reformation*, Whelpley's *Compendium of History*, and Kennett's *Roman Antiquities*.[1]

Early in his novel-writing, moreover, he was aware that the recording of episodes of frontier experience was of potential value as history; in 1873, he made this quite explicit in the preface to *The Mystery of Metropolisville*: "I have wished to make my stories of value as a contribution to the history of civilization in America. If it be urged that this is not the highest function, I reply that it is just now the most necessary function of this kind of literature. Of the value of these stories as works of art, others must judge. . . ." In all his frontier novels except *Metropolisville*, moreover, the setting in time is anterior to his own direct experience—for example, the 1840's for *The End of the World;* the first decade of the nineteenth century for *The Circuit Rider.* In his desire for accuracy, moreover, he had acquired the historian's essential habit of consulting the most reliable contemporary records.

More immediately relevant to the shift to history is the aid and encouragement he gave to his oldest daughter in launching her as a writer. It was one of his beliefs that girls should have careers of their own, whether or not they married. In January, 1878, he first proposed to Lillie that she try writing, and offered to help, even if it meant a reduction in his own income: "I am getting to a time in life," he told her, "when a hard working man of slender constitution ought to have something to fall back on."[2] He wrote this a bare six weeks after his fortieth birthday. By implication, a daughter with an income of her own would be a daughter he would not have to support later on.

His next step was to persuade Dodd, Mead and Company to undertake a series of books to be called *Famous American Indians.* The firm offered a royalty of eight per cent but raised it to ten per cent when Eggleston agreed to be listed as co-author.[3] The result was highly satisfactory: four titles appeared under their joint authorship in the three years 1878-80, and a fifth was added by George Cary Eggleston. *Tecumseh and the Shawnee Prophet,* the critical first in the series, sold out its first printing of twenty-six hundred copies within three months;[4] the publishers were thereby encouraged to continue the series, and the family income was substantially bolstered.

The joint authorship proved to be much more than a device to boost sales, for a good deal of library work was necessary and Eggleston was free to do it as Lillie, with an infant daughter as well as a husband to take care of, was not. As many a graduate student has discovered, research has a peculiar fascination transcending all the drudgery it involves; and, poking about in the New York libraries, Eggleston succumbed. The search for facts about Pocahontas, the subject of their second book, took him to Hakluyt's *Voyages,* to Purchas' *Pilgrims,* and to Neill's *Virginia Company,* in which he found all the letters sent to the company by the Jamestown colonists.[5]

During his book-reviewing days on the *Independent,* Eggleston had become a close friend of Moses Coit Tyler. With his sharpened interest in early American history, he took strong exception to a review in the *Christian Union* of Tyler's new book, *A Study of Our Forefathers,* late in 1878, and badgered the editor to let him write a corrective review.[6] He was rapidly moving toward the fraternity of historians.

As an inevitable corollary, interest in religion, and in his church of Christian Endeavor, receded. Two lively articles he wrote for the *Christian Union,* in November, 1878, and in February, 1879, comprise a kind of valedictory to the preaching profession. Long experience and observation enabled him to catalogue the worst offenses of contemporary clergymen: sanctimonious public behavior, conventional goodness, excessive piety, insincerity and cant, pulpit eccentricity and sensationalism, and the all too common willing acceptance of semi-pauperism. He derided the wearing of special clerical garb to impress a congregation, or as a refuge from reality. Dullness was bad, dishonesty worse, and pedantry the worst sin of all. But congregations committed sins too, especially in their encouragement of false humility and in their intolerance of supposed heretics. Instead of being indignant toward the radicalism of such men as Lyman Beecher and Horace Bushnell, churches, Eggleston believed, should weed out "a few humbugs, clap-trap sensationalists, coxcombs, sanctimonists, self-seekers, parsons who never pay grocery bills, those who write puffs for themselves, and those who carry uncharitableness up to the credit side of the ledger, under the head of zeal." The ministry, he insisted, was the noblest profession a young man could enter; but the despicable behavior of some clergymen was turning it into a sham.[7]

Eggleston did not refer in this catalogue of accumulated complaints to the kind of rift that was growing within the Church of Christian Endeavor, or to his own steady progress toward virtual agnosticism. Early in 1879 he sought to enliven the Sunday evening service with a series called "Newspaper

Topics from a Pulpit Standpoint."[8] It offended certain of the more pious members, and prompted in Eggleston some second thoughts: was that section of Brooklyn a good place for pulpit innovations or, more important, for liberal theology? For his own part, the discussion of current events was one means of avoiding the genuinely religious subject matter that not even the most liberal clergyman could entirely neglect. In the early fall of 1879 he talked with his trustees about resigning; they expressed regret but did not blame him. He recommended as his replacement William McKinley, his old Minnesota friend who could be relied upon to restore the desired degree of orthodoxy.[9]

The church work was hurting their joint literary work, he told Lillie.[10] This was no doubt true, but the statement represented a reshuffling in his list of priorities: authorship had simply crowded theology out of first place. Dizziness, dyspepsia, and other physical discomforts that he reported to his daughter were probably not, as he thought, added reasons for resigning his pulpit; rather, they were concomitants of his impatience to leave once he had decided to.

In the same way, he convinced himself that he needed the relaxation of another trip to Europe; it is more likely that thinking about the trip aggravated his impatience and the attendant physical symptoms. He announced his resignation in mid-December and boarded a steamship almost at once, accompanied by his wife and his two younger daughters, Blanche and Allegra. The departure had none of the fanfare of his first trip; it was flight from a situation that had grown intolerable, but without any clearly seen goal. The decision favoring history took almost a year to form.

## II  *Dead Center*

An interviewer's curiosity in 1897 uncovered what might have been a plausible explanation of Eggleston's shift to history. Pressed for a reason, Eggleston said that in 1879 his wealthy friend Roswell Smith, owner of the Century Company, had offered to advance all the money he might need to write history.[11] If Smith had made such an offer *at that time*, he would have spared Eggleston much of the mental agony attendant upon his resignation from the Brooklyn church and his flight to Europe. George Cary Eggleston, in his memoir *The First of the Hoosiers,* repeated the story but added a new twist: his brother, he said, was too independent to accept the offer.

Eggleston and Smith were as intimate as an intellectual and a successful entrepreneur could ever be; they dined together often and enjoyed rides about New York. But well as he knew Smith, Eggleston never quite understood him: Smith's shrewdness, approaching craftiness in business deals, though he never descended to meanness, would suddenly yield to open-handed generosity; he seemed to find an equal pleasure in making money and in giving it away.[12] To settle a quarrel in 1880, he bought out Josiah Holland's control of *Scribner's Monthly* and renamed it *The Century;* but he did not change the volume numbering.[13] In 1882 he dismayed Eggleston by asking him to write a biography of James Garfield; but Eggleston had more objections than Smith could override.[14] About a year later, when the two men were enjoying the March sun in Central Park, Smith suddenly asked whether Eggleston could write in Europe. It was an easy question to answer. A few days later a check for one thousand dollars arrived in the mail, with the explanation that the Century Company wished to contribute to his expenses while he studied abroad.[15] Despite what George thought later, no excess of independence prevented Edward from taking the money, although he deferred the trip until 1885.

By the time Smith sent the check, he already had concrete assurance that Eggleston could write history, for three essays of a projected series on colonial history had already appeared in the *Century.* Opening the magazine to the entire series, which came to thirteen between 1882 and 1888, was one easy way for Smith to encourage the venture. Despite Eggleston's recollection in 1897, however, Smith did not act early enough to ease the passage through the dead center of uncertainty in the early months of 1880.

Neither Smith nor anybody else could have reduced the sheer labor of becoming an historian. It was a kind of writing basically different from anything else that Eggleston had ever tried; it was also a kind he could never accelerate, even after long practice. With his lack of formal training in history he felt he could never rely on what any other historian, however trustworthy, had written; instead, he imposed upon himself the formidable duty of tracing every fact back to its origin. In time he was able to develop an acquaintance with the major sources of primary information and the most reliable procedures for verification; but confirming an obscure detail might take just as much time and trouble in 1888 as in 1882.

In the fallow period before undertaking his study, he had little idea of what lay ahead; and even partial foreknowledge of the difficulties might have dissuaded him from even beginning. At one point early in his research he was so overwhelmed by the bulk of colonial history that he wished the migrants had stayed in Europe;[16] again, when New England history seemed "a horrible labyrinth," he was pessimistic enough to suppose he might "reach the settlement of Boston in the course of ten or twenty years of work."[17]

Once he had collected and verified all the facts, moreover, the actual writing—early drafts, revision after revision, and final polishing—ate up the hours and weeks. While in Cambridge early in 1883 to investigate the Harvard collections, he was invited to read something at a meeting of St. Botolph's Club—the "brain club," as he called it. He chose a section of a paper on the Indians. One member made the almost predictable comment that Eggleston had done less than justice to the red man; but more annoying was the criticism of Charles Deane, who had retired from business to become the author of respected essays on minute points in colonial history. Deane said there was nothing new in the paper, although it was well constructed. He missed the point, Eggleston thought, that good construction rests on a new perception of established facts: "It is one thing to unearth new facts as Mr. Deane does—it is another to see what the facts collectively amount to, & to mass them so as to carry that impression into the mind of the reader. This is the function of the man of letters in the domain of history."[18]

A few weeks later, John Bach McMaster's *A History of the People of the United States* was an instantaneous popular success. Eggleston supposed that he alone considered it a misfortune. He was afraid that the current public interest in history would not last, and that books such as McMaster's— eminently readable, giving general pictures, and bolstering solid facts with imagination—would reduce if not destroy any reader interest in his own kind of writing, which was based on specific details solidly documented.[19] If McMaster had been an older man, writing in an older tradition of history, his book—actually the first volume of a series of eight that was completed as late as 1913—might not have been so disturbing; but he was fifteen years younger than Eggleston, and he shared his interest in social history. His academic position, in the history department at the University of Pennsylvania, gave him a professional advantage that Eggleston could only envy.

The one advantage that Eggleston had, though he recognized it only dimly, was that he was *not* academically trained. He had no formalized discipline to depart from, no departmental tradition or loyalty to rebel against, no preconceived notions to shed. Intstead, he had a realist's instinctive determination to be faithful to actualities, and a novelist's desire to produce an account of his findings that would be of general interest. His conception of the domain of the man of letters in history is, clearly enough, one of the standard approaches to history; it is recognized among the professionals, and welcomed by serious readers in direct proportion to their ability to distinguish verified truth from invention. What had been catalogued by some critics of Eggleston's fiction as a flaw—his inability to invent—was now an important virtue. His boyhood literalness found its full outlet in his history, although interpretation of the facts and their judicious massing to convey a forceful picture called for his most mature judgment and cumulative skill in writing.

Theoretically, the advantages might have outweighed the handicaps, and yielded something more than the two volumes of social history that support whatever continuing reputation Eggleston has among historians—*The Beginners of a Nation* (1896) and *The Transit of Civilization* (1901). He started late, but he had twenty-two years, a third of his life span, to devote to the project. He would not have been Eggleston, however, if, even with his determination to succeed in history, he had turned completely into an ideal research scholar, so narrowly dedicated to his subject as to be blind and deaf to all else. More than at any other time in his life he did remain reasonably loyal to a single purpose, but he was unable to ignore certain important appeals to his interest; and history suffered. The story of his life after 1880 is, accordingly, dual: the implementation of his ambition to write American history in a new way, and the series of interruptions that slowed his progress and limited the result. Compared with the fifteen years prior to the switch to history, the succeeding years exhibit a notable paucity of separate publications. Each of the historical essays stood for

months of hard work; the wonder is not that his total produc-
tivity dwindled, but that he turned out as many other things
as he did. Between 1880 and his death in 1902, he published
an impressive total of fourteen books—the two volumes of social
history, several textbooks, three novels, and the products of his
collaboration with his daughter Lillie. Several articles on the
copyright question, and two on folk speech in America, illustrate
only two of the divergent interests too strong for him to ignore.
He also found the time to write tributes to such departed friends
or idols as George Eliot and Josiah Holland in 1881, Emma
Lazarus and Henry Ward Beecher in 1887, Lowell in 1891,
Roswell Smith in 1892, Oliver Wendell Holmes in 1894, and
Stevenson in 1895. Half a dozen short stories, and contributions
to such magazine symposia as "Formative Influences" and
"Authors on the Wheel," are typical of the variety of shorter
pieces he wrote in this final third of his life.

Roswell Smith's thousand-dollar check, welcome though it
was in 1883, could hardly support a project that would take
an unknowable number of years to complete. Some of the interruptions, those that can be attributed neither to recurring
periods of ill health when he could not do anything nor to the
various "good causes" he felt impelled to aid, were frankly for
the purpose of making money to live on. Of *The Hoosier School-
Boy,* he remarked, "I'm as tickled as a boy with a new kite.
Didn't expect anything of that little pot-boiler."[20] His two final
novels, *The Graysons* (1888) and *The Faith Doctor* (1891),
both yielded respectable royalties, although neither was written
for the income alone. The real pot-boiler of his career was
the school history that he brought out in 1888, in several forms
that differed only slightly from each other; the sales, over the
next few years, yielded more money than all the rest of his
lifetime earnings and justified his hope of leaving an estate of
more than a hundred thousand dollars. Apart from the satisfaction
of leaving generous sums to his three daughters, however, this
unaccustomed affluence meant little to him; but a very small
part of it ten years earlier might have freed him completely for
his pursuit of history. On the other hand, he might have relaxed
the intensity of his effort, or turned even oftener to his distract-
ing interests.

By the end of January, 1880, Eggleston had begun to recover

from the ordeal of leaving his Brooklyn church, and, in the pleasant (but chilly) village of Villiers-le-bel, near Paris, he was able to consider resuming work. Four ideas attracted him: a novel, a history of Louis XIV, a life of Savonarola, and a popular history of the United States. Visiting the Bibliothèque Nationale, he happened to see a reference to the Duc de Mercoeur, a man whom John Smith had mentioned. It interested him only for the moment; he was not ready to start work. Another day he inspected the Cathedral of St. Denis, where several French kings were buried; but the view from the tower was of more interest than the inscriptions. A request from Berlin to translate *Roxy* into German bemused him: "These echoes of my literary life seem like voices from another world in the seclusion & intellectual inactivity in which I am living now." Moving to Villeneuve in Switzerland did not alter his outlook; it meant mostly a different set of landscapes and human types, although climbing in near-by mountains brought back some of his vigor. By July he was still undecided about the future, and a little pessimistic:

> I find myself in middle life with ambition in a state of relaxation. I've rather lost interest in this thing we call life. One gets so little just appreciation that appreciation seems hardly worth much anyhow. Changes of opinion & change of stand-point have weakened some of the old motives & I haven't yet found out whence my propulsion is to come from. I want to serve the world, but I do not consider my service of so much value to the world as I once did. I would like to write in my own way about many things, but I must write as the world wishes about what the world cares for in order to win bread.[21]

A fortnight later, for no reason apparent to Eggleston, health, ambition, restlessness, and optimism all surged back to normal. Southern Europe, he decided, might do for winter, "but Europe be hanged! There is no place on the green sod so nice as America."[22] With only brief stops in Paris, where he bought fifty-three books, and in London, where he read in the British Museum for two or three hours a day, and where the August air seemed unbearably oppressive,[23] he hurried home. He was impatient to begin what he was already calling his magnum opus.

## III  *The Grand Design*

The regimen that Eggleston set for himself late in December, 1881, and continued when at all possible for the rest of his life, differed markedly from any earlier pattern. He had long been a family man; now suddenly he was a man alone with his wife, and often without even her. His two unmarried daughters, having had their modest grand tour of Europe, took rooms of their own; Blanche was studying the violin, Allegra (or Allee) the arts of illustrating and wood-carving. Eggleston and Lizzie had never lived luxuriously; henceforth they contented themselves with two or three rooms, seldom at the same address for as long as a year, but always as close as possible to a large library, whether in New York, Washington, Cambridge, or abroad. What remained of the old family life centered now at Lake George, where the Egglestons as a rule moved in late spring and stayed, often, until the first snows. But Lake George meant no let-up in work; especially after the stone library was built in 1883, Eggleston maintained the same work schedule he followed in the cities: four hours a day, seven days a week, fifty-two weeks a year.

In "The Owl's Nest Family Book," begun at Lake George in 1883 as a private record, Eggleston made extended entries, in 1886 and in 1889, reviewing his progress. On December 6, 1886, he could write with obvious satisfaction that for six years he had departed only twice from his present schedule—while writing *The Hoosier School-Boy* to raise needed cash, and for three and a half months in Italy, in 1885, when he worked on an early draft of *The Graysons*. In those six years he had published ten historical articles and written four others, one of them ready for the printer. His income from these articles came to about a thousand dollars a year, "as the magazine pays me." At some other work, he knew, he could be earning ten times as much, but he had no regrets except that he could not indulge his generosity to his family. His health was better, and his intellectual horizon had been widened. He was ready, therefore, to get out a volume, even though readers had shown little encouragement. "In four days," he concluded, "I shall be 49 years old. E. E."

The next pause to take stock was three years later—in October, 1889. In one year's time he had written a hundred octavo pages for his volume. Then, when the Appletons asked for a school history in 1887, he had laid the major work aside and concentrated on the other, which appeared in August, 1888, with the title *A History of the United States and Its People*. A year later came *A First Book in American History With Special Reference to the Lives and Deeds of Great Americans*. By now his Lake George bookshelves had much of the source material he needed.[24] Lillie helped by preparing the rough draft, and Allegra provided the illustrations (which she signed Æ). After reporting that the *First Book* was everywhere accounted the most attractive school text ever printed, this 1889 entry closes as follows: "Now whether to return to my work in Social History or to pursue first certain more lucrative enterprises so as to win a competence is the question. E. E."

The question of which course to follow in the 1890's became merely academic three months after he worded it, for his wife's death on January 27, 1890, left him hardly able to do ordinary things, let alone decide his future. Daily routines were suddenly no more than puttering about, killing time; for weeks he was unable to concentrate, or to find in hard work a surcease from his misery. They had been married for thirty-two years, and even short periods of separation had been hard for him to bear.

History was, for the moment, out of the question; but he was able, by April, to write a thousand words a day on his new novel, *The Faith Doctor*. He had a sense of being without a future; the best he might hope for was to live day by day and to absorb himself in the fortunes of his characters. Writing a betrothal scene was painful, but it reminded him of his daughters: "The best an older man can do is to rejoice in the happiness and hope of the young." He tried not to coddle his grief, but rather, if he could not "rejoice in any future, to be content and busy in the present."[25]

Despite all these verbal efforts to console himself, however, he did not regain his former healthy outlook until he remarried in September, 1891. The bride was Frances Goode, of Madison, Indiana, his second cousin once removed, and an excellent choice for a man like Eggleston. Since he had always known her, there was a minimum awkwardness in readjustment. Lizzie had been, especially in the early years of their marriage, something of a mother substitute; Frances, a woman of better education, was more of an intellectual partner. Lizzie had learned how to be helpful in many ways, reading Bancroft's book aloud, for example, and copying his crabbed first drafts in her much more readable script. Frances collected the stories for *Duffels,* in 1893, and was increasingly valuable as Eggleston's powers waned; towards the end she was often his fingers for writing and for correcting proof. In the spring of 1902, when a publisher sent part of a revised school history with numerous editorial changes, it was Frances who took charge. "The book was dry as dust," Eggleston complained in a letter to Lillie. "Frances went to work and exhumed me from under the set forms of the old schoolbooks."[26]

Frances did much of the work in preparing two school readers that the American Book Company published in 1895: *Stories of Great Americans for Little Americans,* for the second grade, and *Stories of American Life and Adventure,* for the third grade. Without such help, Eggleston might not have been able to complete the first volume of his social history, which D. Appleton brought out in November, 1896: *The Beginners of a Nation. A History of the Source and Rise of the Earliest English Settlements in America with Special Reference to the Life and Character of the People.*

This book, together with *The Transit of Civilization* that followed in 1901, complete the grand design—so far as Eggleston was able to finish it before he died—that had begun to take form in 1880. Social history has been for so long a familiar variety of American historical writing, or so familiar an element in our history books, that it is hard to imagine the impact made by *The Beginners of A Nation.* It is something of a paradox that we commonly acknowledge Eggleston's pioneering in realistic fiction with novels, especially the first, that are frankly low in literary value and that we acknowledge the continuing respectability of his two volumes of social history, *as* history, but forget the part they played in pioneering the genre. One obvious explanation is that the two volumes did not complete his plan, whereas other social historians—McMaster among his contemporaries and Fox and Schlesinger subsequently in their *History of American Life*—have covered in many volumes the total range of our history. The meagerness of output is a good reason for not considering Eggleston a great historian, but no reason at all for ignoring his contribution to historiography.

The two volumes do not follow each other in chronological

order but comprise a unit; in this sense they do approach completeness. The first gives the European backgrounds of colonization—what was known about America and the differing forces motivating migration—before reporting the actual planting of specific colonies: Jamestown in Book I; Plymouth and Massachusetts Bay in Book II; Maryland, Rhode Island, and the New England dispersions in Book III. *The Transit of Civilization* explores in detail six facets of the human condition as found among the colonizing groups: the state of seventeenth-century knowledge that they shared with Europeans; medical notions; the stage of development of the English language; contemporary ethical standards; the educational tradition; and the original practices, varying from colony to colony, of the division of land and labor. Few historians have ever devoted so much attention to the particular topics that Eggleston developed. What makes his work incomplete, within this range of coverage, is the absence of comparable detail for the non-English migrating groups—the Dutch in New Netherlands, for example, and the Swedes and Finns along the lower Delaware. The story of English migration is itself incomplete, moreover; for, apart from an occasional reference, Eggleston did not reach the time of later English settlements in Georgia and Pennsylvania.

What he was able to do, however, in the two decades he devoted to these two volumes was remarkable enough when we consider the particular approach he adopted. Until the 1870's, historiography had been the avocation of gentlemen—Parkman, Motley, Prescott—who were not interested in the commonplaces of colonial beginnings; or the solid work of men like George Bancroft who felt impelled to interpret the past in aggressively nationalistic terms; or, most common of all, the minutely detailed attention of antiquarians to local history, such as that of towns and parishes. The growth of graduate training after the Civil War and the sudden academic impulse to establish sound method led to the stress on accumulating facts that is quite properly called "scientific history." In his own method, Eggleston acknowledged the scientific (or German) school; the outer margins of both his volumes, in addition to providing a running outline of subheadings, indicate sources of specific statements or give number references to more extensive "Elucidations" following each chapter which are often as sprightly as the text itself. Apart from this meticulous documentation, however, Eggleston was simply not the kind of man who could be satisfied with letting accumulated fact speak for itself; his novelist's interest in character and motive conditioned him to view the early settlers not as pegs on a board but as living beings responding to stimuli and sharing normal emotional reactions.

Francis Parkman had once remarked to Eggleston, "You are the only man in America that can write a history of the United States; you are the only man who has seen so many forms of our life."[27] What Parkman meant was not that Eggleston had been everywhere, for he hadn't; the Far West and the Deep South were outside his direct experience. But he had lived in three major regions—Middle West, tidewater South, the Northeast—long enough to know them intimately as a resident and not as a visitor; and the first of these areas may be divided into three, quite different ones—the Ohio Valley, the Minnesota frontier, and Chicago. Nowhere had he seen a dynastic carving up of history; instead, he had observed steady social change transforming entire communities. The rate of change differed—Vevay and Amelia were almost static; Minnesota and Illinois, exhilaratingly dynamic—but it was the people everywhere, in groups—not individual leaders, not even great dramatic events—that shaped the emerging culture. He early formed the notion that American civilization, at any given moment, was the result of unbroken evolution from the colonial beginnings.

In his initial conception of his grand design, he had jotted down some of the chapters he hoped to write; one cause for regret is that he did not live to report "The Great Kentucky Revival" (which he barely alluded to in *The Circuit Rider*) or "Early Fur Traders" or "The Old Gentry in the South."[28] The very breadth of his concept, seldom equalled by other historians, severely limited what he could do; one man, working alone, would have needed several lifetimes to present the complete story of the evolving American civilization. One significance of his work was the model it provided for younger historians who, collectively, could trace the orderly story in its many facets, decade by decade, region by region. Long before his death he realized how little he could do of the conjectural total. He had to be content with that little, and with the solid satisfaction of having done it well.

## IV  *Perquisites of Fame*

Completion of *The Beginners of a Nation* was the most satisfying fact of Eggleston's life; the publication date, November 20, 1896, was his day of days. In the 1880's he had sometimes felt that his historical essays were finding no readers at all; now that the same material, reworked and refined, had appeared between the solid covers of a book, the response astonished him. For weeks his desk was flooded with letters of congratulation from writers and editors, from other historians, from friends he had known years before and had almost forgotten, from perfect strangers, and from relatives. Jennie wrote from Evanston with touching naiveté, "I am *so* glad you were born!"[29] Joe said he'd enjoyed the book but was sorry that Edward didn't share his hatred of New Englanders "so that he might give them some deserved digs in return for the many they have given us."[30] It was impossible, of course, to please everyone; for, as will be seen, some of the reviewers complained that the book was far too critical of the Puritans and too favorable to Virginia.

The Authors' Club turned its next meeting into a reception in his honor; McMaster's presence struck Eggleston as a most magnanimous gesture. Weir Mitchell and Charles Dudley Warner also came from a distance, and cordial messages were read from Justin Winsor, Moses Coit Tyler, and Herbert B. Adams.[31] By the following January 24 he was still in the clouds but a little embarrassed at the continuing adulation; club cronies who had always argued with him now treated him as an oracle or as some kind of historical souvenir. Autograph hunters besieged him. Editors begged for articles. He was suddenly a famous man.

He had been famous before, in a meteoric, sensational way, when *The Hoosier School-Master* caught the excited attention of readers and nonplussed the critics. Its success, as astonishing to him as to anybody else, had justified his deliberate decision to become an author; but his satisfaction then had been accompanied by a clear awareness that the book was hurriedly written and far short of literary art. He had set out, in subsequent novels, to overcome the faults that were all too obvious to him once the reviewers had pointed them out, but even with steady improvement he had never repeated his first success. That initial fame hung over him like some dark angel; it came to be a restrictive element, one that he tried in vain to throw off.

The new fame was altogether different. It was the result, not of a lucky accident, but rather of an arduous process that gradually gave final form to an idea hazily seen sixteen years earlier. If *The Hoosier School-Master* had its forerunners in two or three slight stories with a Vevay setting, *The Beginners of a Nation* had thirteen sturdy advance scouts in the series of historical essays in the *Century*. Eggleston joined the Authors' Club as one of its founders in 1882, eleven years after he brought out his first novel; during the major period of his fiction writing he had slight contact with other authors, no concrete sense of belonging to a profession. By the time the *Beginners* was issued, in contrast, he had been for a dozen years a member of the American Historical Association, attending meetings and taking an active part in its activities. He was, in fact, one of its organizing members at Saratoga in 1884. He had rubbed shoulders and exchanged opinions with most of the nation's professional historians. At the 1890 meeting he had declared that "American institutions were all historical developments from colonial germs,"[32] a revolutionary assertion that turned the focus of critical attention from Teutonic to native origins. From this and other statements, his colleagues in the profession had a fairly explicit notion of what it was he proposed to do and could judge the book, as some of them did in reviews, on the basis of that foreknowledge. Some of the sharpest criticism came from members of this group, but the general applause from his academic colleagues, serving as a nucleus for the broader popular approval, made this resurgence of fame far more welcome to him, and more meaningful, than the shallow, casual, virtually unearned and often resented fame as author of *The Hoosier School-Master*.

The reviews give a cross section not only of critical opinion of the book but also of contemporary opinion in general. The great number of newspapers, many more than in the mid-twentieth century, permitted a wide variety of criticism; reviews reached Eggleston from ten Boston papers, for example, and from four in Brooklyn—*Eagle, Citizen, Life,* and *Times.* The *Eagle* described his style as "crisp, pungent, idiomatic, and withal graceful," and observed that subjecting the Puritans to ordinary criticism would, not many years before, have seemed

a profanation.[33] The Brooklyn *Life,* in contrast, concluded that
Eggleston's Virginia ancestry and Southern prejudice prevented
his seeing all sides of New England's complex struggle to found
a state, and it criticized his condemnation of the persecutors of
Anne Hutchinson without showing how her teachings threatened
to stir up civil strife.[34] The Boston reviewers were not distressed
by his severity toward such Puritan leaders as John Endicott.
Since Eggleston cast Roger Williams as a major hero, Providence
opinions of the book were lofty. To the reviewer for the Philadelphia Press, however, Eggleston's devoting one of the book's
ten chapters to Williams seemed disproportionate when he totally
ignored New York and Pennsylvania; but the Puritan bigotry
deserved the strong language Eggleston applied to it—an opinion
no doubt reflecting at long remove the ancient Quaker bitterness
toward Massachusetts Bay.[35]

One review certain to be friendly was George Cary Eggleston's
in the New York *World.*[36] It was high time, George thought, for
truthful historians to explode the self-deluding notion that the
first settlers were of the gentility. The Baltimore *Sun* commented
on the same point but in a less friendly way: "We all agree that
the first settlers of Virginia were a thriftless lot, but no one
has pictured them quite as worthless as Mr. Eggleston."[37] In
distant San Francisco, the *Report* expressed delight at this
social reduction of the first settlers: "It turns out these ancestors
were very common. There was hardly a streak of blue blood
through them all."[38]

Iconoclasm was frequently charged against Eggleston. The
Brooklyn *Citizen* ended a very long review by expressing a
certain dread of the direction historians seemed to be heading:
"the cold and rigid processes of history make sad work of many
traditions, overturn the most cherished figures of fancy and
reduce not a few whom we had fashioned in heroic mold to
images of every common clay."[39] Nobody thought the style
was cold, however; Richard Henry Stoddard's comment was
typical of many: "Mr. Eggleston writes with spirit, with humor,
and with just enough picturesqueness to vivify his narrative."[40]

The *Critic* objected that Eggleston was preoccupied with the
English settlers, as if England only were the origin of our country
and the center of the world: "When shall we be delivered from
the bondage of this notion?"[41] The *Congregationalist,* of Boston,
cited minute errors as evidence of a "conspicuous carelessness";

for example, Eggleston had said that Forefathers' Day was December 10 instead of the eleventh.[42] Paul Leicester Ford, in the *Book Buyer,* felt that Eggleston failed to grasp the vital core of Puritanism and preferred to ridicule its absurdities. At the rate of this first volume, Ford estimated, *A History of Life in the United States* would require fifty volumes.[43] The most hostile review was in Eggleston's own former journal, the *Independent;* the critic objected to the "barren, negative, fault-finding harping on the minor points, accidents and non-essentials of the history which no respectable historian has been guilty of for fifty years or more, and which we hoped was now forever impossible."[44]

But Eggleston had not expected total approval, and the preponderance of good opinion was highly gratifying. William P. Trent's ten-page pre-publication review in the *Forum*[45] had been particularly welcome; numerous reviewers in lesser periodicals also welcomed it—and cribbed from it without shame. One of the most interesting opinions was the one printed in the Rochester *Post-Express*: "We are not a little shocked by the deductions, though there is no reason to believe that they are erroneous. The trouble is that we have been wrongly educated. Our historical instruction has been along the lines of idealization." More men like Eggleston and Woodrow Wilson were needed to dispel the glamor that had long hidden the truth.[46] A reviewer in upstate New York capped the praise by saying that this was a book to buy, beg, borrow, or steal, and that there never had been such a bargain—four hundred excellent pages for a mere $1.50.[47]

Any author is pleased when critics generally accept his intention as worth while and his book as fulfilling that intention. Four years later, shortly before his second volume appeared, Eggleston publicly stated his philosophy of history in his presidential address to the American Historical Association at its 1900 convention in Detroit. By titling it "The New History" he acknowledged the opinion of various responsible historians that it *was* new, a fresh departure; the term is still sometimes applied to other works that stress the social side of history. "For five hundred years," he wrote, "nearly every historical writer has felt it necessary to touch his cap in a preface to Herodotus and Thucydides," but Thucydides stuck to wars and gave no information about Aristophanes, Sophocles, or Phidias.

(The word "war," incidentally, appears in the index of neither of Eggleston's two volumes.) So also with Herodotus and Tacitus: "Let us brush aside once and for all the domination of the classic tradition." As for great political figures (again, minimized in the two volumes), Eggleston inclined toward Tolstoi's view of the leader as little more than the figurehead of a broad popular movement; as between the leader and the movement, Eggleston thought the movement much worthier of study.

Preparing this address, as he was, just after the war with Spain, which he had vigorously protested, he pulled out all the stops in condemning the attention to war so prominent in most history books. It was the object of history, he believed, to cultivate out of people their fascination with the brute and the hero, and with the carnage they caused; historians had a responsibility to teach "the wisdom of diplomacy, the wisdom of avoidance—in short, the fine wisdom of arbitration, that last fruit of human experience." A little further on he broadened this judgment: "The main object of teaching history is to make good men and women, cultivated and broad men and women." But historians had no right to leave unsaid what might be offensive—the fact, for instance, that many an ancestress of Colonial Dames was sold off the ship upon arrival. Such selectivity was George Bancroft's practice, and "That is why his volumes stand in undisturbed repose on the shelves where are those books which no gentleman's library is complete without." Better models for modern historians were Raleigh, with his *History of the World;* Macaulay, with his intimate description of old-time London; Green, despite the inaccuracies of his *Short History;* DeTocqueville; and, among the still living, Lord Bryce (to whom *The Beginners of a Nation* is inscribed).

Eggleston closed his address with three confident predictions for the new century: that it would produce better histories, that more history would be written about people, and that the 1900's would *be* better, since every age is a little better than the preceding. The first two predictions have come true; the third must remain a matter of opinion. Knowing Eggleston's own history, the address offers no surprises. History as a means of improving people is consistent with a long career as preacher and Sunday school man. But overriding all else is his central philosophy of history: people are what count, not famous persons. It is the same way of thinking that made him immediately responsive to Taine's advocacy of artistic attention to the local and the commonplace.

After preparing his presidential address, Eggleston was too ill to read it, or even to attend the annual meeting. He had learned to live with recurring illness, but, as he entered his sixties, his ability to recover from any given attack declined. By early 1899 the prospect of not completing his second volume was a distressing one. He wrote to Lillie: "It will be 1901 before my book will see the light and it will probably be my last tho' Frances does not believe I can quit work while I live. I can not go on writing long with sleep so broken. But I am enjoying what I do though I am mortally slow."[48] His increasing preoccupation with his own health reduced his apparent concern over the welfare of his daughters and his interest in their affairs; and they felt varying degrees of resentment. Also his growing nervousness among people, especially lively youngsters like his grandchildren, kept him away from Lake George; living quietly with Frances, in Madison or in hotel rooms in New York, was the one way he could hope to work. But the resulting alienation from his family was a sorry price to pay; moreover, his awareness of it reduced his efficiency.

The second volume of his social history, *The Transit of Civilization*, won the same favorable approval as the first from the general periodicals, but in the scholarly journals it was generally considered inferior. Barrett Wendell, in the *American Historical Review*, thought it was confused, bewildering, misleading—the result of mental indigestion from too much browsing in libraries —and lacking in "imaginative sympathy with the human spirit of the times."[49] Charles M. Andrews, a specialist in colonial history, wrote the most adverse of all the reviews in the *Political Science Quarterly*: *The Transit*, he thought, reflected poor organization, an unscientific approach, and lamentably out-dated scholarship; the six essay-chapters were no better than "a kaleidoscopic assortment of notes, lengthy, discursive and often bewildering."[50]

Within a decade, Andrews softened his judgment; Eggleston's two volumes, he decided in 1911, comprised "an admirable and novel work," delightfully written. Although the first book was the sounder, the second contained "a number of valuable chapters on out-of-the-way subjects."[51] It is no doubt best to view the two as a unit; considering the second alone, without the first which it complements, might easily bewilder a reviewer.

If that reviewer, or a modern reader, looks for a continuous narrative, or the customary chronological progress, he will not find it; part of the peculiar fascination of *The Transit* springs from its division into topical essays. Our conjectural modern reader may expect to share the regret of the critics that Eggleston did not live to extend the series.

Dying on September 3, 1902—barely a year after *The Transit of Civilization* was published—Eggleston had little time to be disappointed about its scholarly reception. It was a real satisfaction just to be able to complete it. A few more years, could he have had them, would have permitted him to provide a broader base for critical judgment. But in 1937 Michael Kraus spoke of the "charm and coherence" of Eggleston's volumes and of their strong influence on younger historians;[52] A. M. Schlesinger in the *Encyclopedia of Social Sciences*[53] compared Eggleston and McMaster in their common devotion to social history, but he found Eggleston's work more philosophical, less political, better digested, and more graceful. It seems reasonable to predict that the final judgment of Eggleston as an historian will approximate the opinions of Kraus and Schlesinger.

## CHAPTER 6

# One Kind of American

## I  *The War Feeling*

THE WAR WITH SPAIN was a source of great chagrin to
Eggleston, not only for the reasons shared by many people
of conscience and good will but for reasons peculiarly his own.
It cast doubt on his thesis of orderly advance from Colonial
origins and, by extension, on the grand scheme he had given
a quarter of a century to bring to maturity. And it was a cruel
caprice of timing; his final effort, the production of his second
volume, was forced to coincide with a period of blood-lust
irrationality. Given the circumstances, it was a mistake for him
to move late in 1897 to Washington for research in the Library
of Congress; it placed him in the very center of a jingoistic
whirlwind. By the following April he was completely disgusted.
"I am very tired," he wrote to Lillie, "living alongside Congress
with its daily stupidities in a critical time. We are going to
war but people can't agree just what it is we mean to fight
about." He put the blame on "the confounded little big men
and the damnable big little newspapers."[1] To Herbert B. Adams,
who asked him to speak to a seminar at the Johns Hopkins
University, he confided: "Living right at the door of Congress
in this tiresome time I don't seem to care much for American
citizenship; . . . the study of history with reference to it has
made half a nation of irrational jingoes." He wished he might
"get away from the howl of the congressman & the news-
boy. . . ."[2] But when he did go away to New York for medical
care, he found the people there equally preoccupied with the
news from Cuba.

One recent critic of Eggleston as an historian, in an attempt
to explain why the *Transit* is weaker than the *Beginners*,
observed that in the later volume "history became a collection

of colorful details interlarded with the judgments of a tolerant, kindly personality."[3] The interlardings, it may be noted in passing, suggest the asides that appear often in Eggleston's novels and that are traceable back to the early habit, in his preaching, of reviewing ideas drawn from his current reading. All the novels employ the omniscient third person, a narrative point of view that permits—and in the nineteenth century commonly encouraged—intrusive first-person remarks by the author. Whether a similar technique in historical writing pleases or offends depends on the way we want our history to be; but the mere marshalling of facts for the reader to grasp and interpret was a kind of history that Eggleston deliberately rejected.

The tolerance and kindliness mentioned by the recent critic were traits that deserve examination. For all the acerbities toward the Puritans that several reviewers noted in the *Beginners*, Eggleston was, at heart and always, generous in judgment and behavior. His bitterness over the war with Spain was not that of a cynic but rather that of an idealist who feels betrayed by events. His political idealism had shown itself earlier, not in 1872 or 1876, when he was still too much engrossed in fiction and liberal theology to join the Liberal Republicans opposed to Grantism, but in 1884, when he permitted a letter he wrote to be published as a pamphlet, *Blaine vs. Cleveland*, by the National Committee of Republicans and Independents. He simply felt that Blaine's record of corruption disqualified him for the presidency. A similar attitude underlay an opinion of Harrison given privately in 1891: "This Harrison machine is the pettiest I have ever known."[4]

Cleveland, to his gratification, proved to be an even better President than he had hoped, and he told him so more than once. As a strong Lincoln man during the Civil War, Eggleston could not, probably, have changed his party label afterwards; but political idealism permits a preference for Presidents of the party opposing one's own with no sense of being either disloyal or illogical. The note Eggleston sent just before Cleveland retired from office must, in any event, have been very welcome: "Now on Washington's birthday as your public career draws to a glorious close you will let me once again say to you that yours is one of the great presidencies. I do not know any greater according to the opportunities." Future public officers, Eggleston concluded, would be proud to be compared with Cleveland.[5]

By leaving office just when he did, Cleveland escaped the pressure put upon McKinley to force Spain out of Cuba. In the idealistic way of thinking, conducting a war for that purpose was bad enough; the evil was compounded by the high mortality among recruits in army camps. Recalling the miseries he had helped to alleviate in 1866 by his work for the North-West Sanitary Fair, Eggleston sent McKinley a strong letter of protest: "Alger," he declared, "is a slaughter-pen without purpose." The President, a secretary replied, was equally distressed.[6] By this time Eggleston had retired with Frances to Madison, Indiana, where the war seemed remote. Left alone, he found he could forget Cuba and work at his former level; he even regained some of the weight he had lost.

## II  *New Loyalties*

An ideal scholar may be one who can pursue his research and writing undistracted by events around him, however raucous or alarming. Eggleston fell short of this standard; he had too lively a conscience and too strong a humanitarian zeal to hold aloof when good causes needed support or bad ones needed to be condemned. He also liked people. Retiring to Madison—increasingly his winter habit in his final years—benefited his health and enabled him to work, but he was aware, ruefully, that part of the price was giving up the familiar intimate associations of his clubs. He missed the gatherings at the Authors' Club, the good talk around the fire at the Century, the chance to make new friends at the Cosmos Club in Washington. Here he met General Greeley, the Arctic explorer; and a "gentle deprecating elderly gentleman" who proved to be John G. Nicolay, Lincoln's secretary; and Hamlin Garland, who was eloquent about *The Hoosier School-Master* as a milestone in his own progress toward a writing career.[7] George Cary Eggleston, describing the Authors' Club Watch Night that ushered in the year 1899, called it the best ever, despite a blizzard; and he said that many members asked about Edward[8]—a small measure of solace for not being able to attend.

But even in the remoteness of southern Indiana Eggleston could make new friends. Meredith Nicholson, born in Indiana but living in Denver, wrote about his progress on a book to be called *The Hoosiers;* when it appeared in 1900, it had the benefit of details provided by Eggleston as their correspondence length-ened. It was gratifying to Eggleston to discover that somebody shared his high regard for the cultural attainments of the Middle West, especially those of the older Ohio River communities.[9] If, as he now feared, he would never have the time to complete an autobiography, it was important to get the facts right in books and in articles that other men might produce. Lucien V. Rule of Goshen, Kentucky, also opened a correspondence. He cared only for realism, he said, adding that "you are the head of that in America." Not even Hawthorne, he thought, had written more penetratingly about men's religious instincts. In the autobiography that he urged Eggleston to write, he hoped for total candor about his liberation from narrow orthodoxy.[10]

Another friendship, begun at Lake George and continued by letter, was with Obadiah Cyrus Auringer, who subsequently issued the only poetic tribute to Eggleston: *Friendship's Crown of Verses; being Memorials of Edward Eggleston* (1907). There were also a good many letters from strangers conveying thanks for *The Hoosier School-Master;* people were prompted to reread this book, or to read it for the first time, by the resurgence of fame that *The Beginners of a Nation* occasioned. One such letter was from the superintendent of the House of the Lord Mission in New York; he and his wife had read the novel aloud, he reported, and had particularly appreciated Bud Means's experience with the Church of the Best Licks.[11] Testimonials of this nature were very welcome in the late 1890's, for pessimism over the war had produced in Eggleston the hope that people would forget his personal existence and remember only his books. By 1900 he no longer resented the enduring popularity of his first book; the numerous unsolicited letters praising it were a warrant that at least one book of his would endure.

The new friendship that Eggleston most enjoyed in this period was with John Livingston Lowes, whom he visited in his home on the lovely hilltop campus of Hanover College, near Madison and overlooking the Ohio River. When Frances gave Lowes a copy of *Sister Tabea,* a story set in the Dunkard Convent in Ephrata, Pennsylvania, Lowes expressed the wish that it might be translated into German so that it could reach an audience that would certainly be appreciative. Later he sent Frances a German edition of *The End of the World.*[12] Eggleston respected the promise of scholarship that he detected in Lowes, who for his own part was grateful for the encouragement of a man whose scholarly career was nearing its close.

In his early wanderings, Eggleston did not pause to consider the effect his moving might have on his circle of friends. Revisiting Indiana during his Minnesota decade, he was consumed with self-pity when he walked the familiar streets and met only strangers. Later, on a lecture trip in Minnesota in 1875, nine years after the move to Illinois, he grieved to find so few people he had known. The only colleague in the state Methodist Conference with whom he kept in close touch was William McKinley, who succeeded him in the pulpit of the Church of Christian Endeavor and who subsequently, in his *History of Minnesota Methodism* (1911), described the Eggleston of 1857 in intimate and complimentary terms. The erosion of fame, down to the bedrock of durability, is sometimes attended by just this sort of coincidence—the one friend not lost track of becoming the recorder of circumstances that could easily have been forgotten. Once Eggleston became well known, such accidents of friendship were less important to the survival of information and opinion.

Wherever he was, Eggleston made friends easily, by nature liking people unless and until there was some good reason for not liking them. Two exceptions to this general statement were visiting English authors for whom the Authors' Club gave receptions: Matthew Arnold and Edmund Gosse. Listening to Arnold lecture on Emerson, Eggleston thought he spoke "as if he had a mouth full of mush, or badly fitting false teeth." But Mrs. Arnold made up for him; she struck Eggleston as clever, interesting, and unassuming.[13] Gosse he described as "egotistical, pretentious & superficial," saying "calculatedly flattering things in an English drawl"; and Mrs. Gosse, sad to report, offered nothing in compensation.[14]

Most other Englishmen, however, made quite a different impression on Eggleston: Lord Bryce, who did his best to secure permission for him to see the Percy manuscripts; the London bookseller Quaritch, who, learning of Lillie's interest in Columbus, insisted on giving Eggleston a collected edition of Columbus letters, priced at two guineas, to take to her;[15] Sir Walter Besant and Andrew Lang, and Austin Dobson, who seemed to Eggleston "to have something very charming in his talk";[16] George McDonald, the pious Scottish novelist whose family enacted *Pilgrim's Progress* at a Portman Square town house;[17] and, best of all, Robert Louis Stevenson, in New York on his way to the South Seas, who praised Eggleston's experience on the frontier and his courage in writing about it, and who referred to his sailing on Lake George as something with an element of risk and therefore worth doing.[18]

Toward younger writers, Eggleston was always friendly and generous; sometimes he volunteered a boost to reputation. Bliss Perry, joining the Authors' Club in 1894, never forgot his genial kindliness.[19] Booth Tarkington had a somewhat different experience: when Howells and Eggleston visited the Lantern Club, which Tarkington had just joined, he was ordered to sing for them, to his acute embarrassment. But in 1908, at a Lotos Club dinner, Tarkington seconded Garland's statement that "Edward Eggleston was the father of us all" with the comment, "You are perfectly right. He was."[20] The best single example of encouragement was a note that Eggleston sent to young Edwin Arlington Robinson and a follow-up comment in an interview: "A man in Gardiner, Maine, has written lately some delightfully original little bits of verse and printed them in a little blue pamphlet. . . . He calls it 'The Torrent and the Night Before.'"[21] In a letter expressing his appreciation, Robinson made the comment, which was no doubt true, that such unsolicited praise was more gratifying than a man in Eggleston's position could easily realize.[22]

The emphasis on the native origins of American development in *The Beginners of a Nation* has led one Eggleston critic to suggest that his democracy was of the pioneers, not of the urban proletariat.[23] It is necessarily true that in never getting out of the seventeenth century Eggleston had no occasion, as an historian, to discuss the effect of latter-day migrations; but the corollary cannot fairly be drawn that he lacked sympathy for newer elements in the population. In 1881 he and Lizzie heard Felix Adler talk on radicalism, and Eggleston described him as slight, intellectual, young, "a George Eliot sort of a Jew! . . . We both think him a manly fellow with the courage of his convictions."[24] A few weeks later, Eggleston met, at Richard Watson Gilder's "quaint and pretty house," a Miss Schuyler, of *the* Schuylers and thereby a scion of one of the earliest migrant groups in America, the New Amsterdam Dutch. Her obvious pride in both her family and her heirlooms prompted one of the most unflattering descriptions that Eggleston ever confided to a lettter.[25] This was hardly an instance of a poor man's inverted snobbery, for he numbered several wealthy men among his close friends— Roswell Smith, Andrew Carnegie (the Authors' Club "angel"), and Isador Straus of the famous mercantile family. All of these were "doers," like Eggleston himself, and interested in some of the same ideas and causes. What drew Eggleston and Straus together was their common admiration for Grover Cleveland, whom both supported actively (though for different reasons— Straus was a Gold Democrat) in his campaigns for the Presidency.

But though he often had dinner with Isador, Eggleston formed a closer friendship with his younger brother Oscar, a lawyer, diplomat, and writer; his book *Roger Williams, the Pioneer of Religious Liberty* (1894) was one that Eggleston could particularly appreciate. In the fall of 1896 he proposed Oscar for membership in the Century Club. Eleven years earlier, he had proposed Brander Matthews for the Century, only to discover a certain prejudice against adding more writers.[26] Straus was at least as eminently qualified as Matthews except on the one point that seemed to matter. If Eggleston had not been fully aware of the virulence of anti-Semitism in New York, he learned it now. His close friends among the club members responded enthusiastically when he sounded them out—W. W. Appleton and Laurence Hutton in particular, and George Haven Putnam, who expressed the hope that no medieval prejudice would bar so good a citizen, scholar, and man. Gilder held aloof; he was still smarting, he explained, from the "black eye" he had recently suffered when a candidate of his own was rejected. Through it all, Straus was serenely good-natured. He said he wouldn't mind being black-balled as one of the tribe of Abraham, but by the next April he asked that his name be withdrawn: a final test would be unpleasant even if he passed.[27]

In the summer of 1893, Eggleston had learned of an Edward Eggleston Literary Society that had been organized the year before in Manhattan's Public School 22. The corresponding secretary was Isador Kresel, who had been born in Austria in 1878 and who had come to the United States in 1890; he kept Eggleston informed of the club's activities, and invited him to attend the first open meeting in his honor, on November 26, at Congress Hall on Stanton Street.[28] He might bring any friends he wished; he chose Lee Kohns, Oscar Straus's nephew, to keep him "in countenance," as he wrote to Lillie that night, "among the Children of Israel." The members read essays and engaged in debating. "The poor little fellows were much encouraged. They had gone to the expense of a carriage to take me over there. I shall send them some of my books."[29] The letter of thanks from Kresel resembles Robinson's of four years later; Eggleston could not imagine what an impression his presence had made.[30] The society continued for several years, and Eggleston's interest remained active.

Eight years later, at an Author's Club reception for President Low of Columbia, Low spoke of a certain lad aided by a Pulitzer scholarship who had just been named an aide to fearless new District Attorney William Travers Jerome. Straus, next morning, learned that it was Kresel, and he relayed to Eggleston the young man's insistence that he owed everything to Eggleston's early help and encouragement.[31]

If to the foregoing we add Eggleston's interest in Emma Lazarus and the tribute he wrote when she died,[32] it might seem logical to postulate that the Jewish element of the urban proletariat had a special attraction for Eggleston. A more reasonable conclusion is that he was a man above prejudice, judging people after he met them, not before, and looking for the best in them. If any prejudice is evident in his fiction, it is the rather obvious sympathy, sentimentally presented, for the virtuous underprivileged, and a corresponding antipathy for wealthy villains—such as Jack Means, Mr. Plausaby, Captain Lumsden. The young protagonists come out the winners in the unequal contest but not, in the rags-to-riches formula of the dime novels, by becoming rich themselves. This naïve conflict is missing in the later novels, but in the last of them all, *The Faith Doctor,* wealth is presented as a dubious commodity if not a positive curse: "the man who had been a blithe youth but twenty years before becomes the possessor of an uneasy tumor he calls a fortune." Eggleston seemed unable to decide which he pitied more, the scion of old wealth who imagines he is superior to the self-made man, or the self-made man himself who, lacking a background in culture, proves a social boor and bore.

In an 1875 essay on Josiah Holland, Eggleston remarked that moralizing of the sort found in Holland's novels appealed to the healthy core of American society.[33] Without ever defining this "healthy core," Eggleston made it clear, on various occasions, that what he meant was not Whitman's *en-masse,* but the great middle class which, until about 1880, was statistically a majority of the American population—rural and small-town families long in the land, who were economically self-sufficient, Protestant, Republican, conservative, conventional, relatively immobile, provincial in outlook, and who were suspicious of immigrants, Catholics, Democrats, big cities, new ideas, and change. Eggleston was a product of that dominant class; so were most of the people he knew or had anything to do with, his minority friends excepted. As a reformer and a pioneer, however, and also as an artist and an intellectual, he could succeed only by freeing himself from the limitations of this class. The supposedly superior virtues of the class made breaking away from it a difficult and sometimes a long, slow process—harder in certain ways than the escape of a newly arrived American from an ethnic "ghetto" in lower Manhattan.

Part of the difficulty stemmed from an ineradicable sense of never quite being able to leave the dominant class. But if Eggleston respected his "healthy core" in theory, in practice he found it increasingly uncongenial. Its behavior could sometimes outrage him—when, for example, editors wanted to tone down *Roxy,* or when he failed to get Oscar Straus into the Century Club. It could also bore him—as he grew easily bored with unresponsive congregations in Minnesota or with his too conventional congregation in Brooklyn. Certain occasions and incidents helped him realize how wide the gap had grown between his values and those of the respectable majority. In the summer of 1893 he consented to be a lecturer at Chautauqua in western New York. The experience on the final day yielded this report to one of his daughters:

This is Recognition Day. All the graduates new and old are marching in processions preceded by a great line of little girls in double column and white dresses. They will all go by here presently in a grand procession to the Hall of Philosophy, a white wooden Parthenon open on all sides. There the new-fledged graduates will march under symbolical arches and there will be no end of nonsense. . . . The grand procession has just gone by while the chimes are ringing and the bands braying. The dignitaries counter marched through the open columns just here and were applauded by the Chautauqua handkerchief signal—then the graduates went through in the same style. Now the procession fades from view with the chimes ringing "My Country 'tis of thee" "Nearer my God to thee" and "Auld Lang Syne," while Frances is quite unable to restrain her sense of the utter ludicrousness of such a way of getting knowledge. I was asked to march with the *other* dignitaries but I just couldn't.[34]

Many of the reforming and pioneering activities that Eggleston threw himself into, sometimes to the detriment of his major ambitions, were of a sort that could not alarm or alienate conventional people. Some reactionaries resisted the Sunday school movement, but it had the support of respected church leaders in most of the Protestant denominations, and it had the obvious virtue of conditioning youngsters for lifelong loyalty to organized religion. As a relatively new movement, moreover, it lacked any strongly entrenched principles for a brash newcomer to attack at his peril; the lively suggestions that Eggleston made, in his editorials and his addresses to conventions, were generally welcomed as hints for gaining success comparable to his own.

Conditions were much the same in the kindergarten movement, which was opposed in some quarters but never as being dangerously radical. Organizing a private kindergarten in his own Evanston home caused considerable eyebrow raising; but at the worst his action seemed merely eccentric. Eggleston's easy appeal to youngsters, complementing the skill he acquired as a preacher and popular lecturer, was a great advantage; other men, such as Horace Bushnell, might work out the logic of Christian Nurture but could never put it to the practical test as Eggleston was able to. It would be difficult to assess the contribution he made to the firm establishment of Sunday schools and kindergartens in the United States, largely because he drifted away so soon to the pursuit of quite different interests.

Eggleston's exposures in the Chicago *Tribune* of horrifying conditions in Illinois prisons and poor-houses were a much more serious reform effort, but they were not long maintained, and were rather weakened by his device of hiding behind a pseudonym. Fictional application of the same reforming protests was probably more effective, though he never carried the point as far as Dickens did, or Charles Reade; and he was never a thesis novelist like Edward Bellamy. *The Faith Doctor* may be taken as a veiled attack on Christian Science. The only theme in one of his novels that seemed really controversial in its time, though hardly so today, is the infidelity-forgiveness sequence in *Roxy*. More important than any particular theme in the novels, of course, is the pioneering in realism itself which they represent collectively and which cannot be discounted even by those who deprecate their level of artistry.

In his first novels, Eggleston, consciously or not, catered to the conventional expectations of his "healthy core of society." In *The Graysons*, however, he deliberately avoided a happy ending; by 1887, apparently, he had seen too much of life to be able any longer to write "poetic justice" into his fiction. The book has a further interest as a key to his mental evolution in revealing a lessened sympathy with the frontier. The courtroom crowd, for example, exhibits a repellingly morbid interest in anatomical details. For the first time, moreover, the complex of frontier religion is presented in an unfavorable light. Earlier, Eggleston had always balanced a religious hypocrite with a sincere churchman; in *The Graysons* the one overtly religious man is the villain.

As if to make his disaffection with religious orthodoxy unmistakably explicit, Eggleston in this same year (1887) publicly asserted his acceptance of nineteenth-century scientific thought. In his youth he had been particularly fond of Thomas à Kempis. "But reading à Kempis is like saying one's prayers in a crypt." Now he kept the book on a high shelf, out of reach, preferring to "walk in wide fields with Charles Darwin."[35]

## III  *The Fight for Copyright*

The Century Club, which Eggleston joined in the fall of 1883, served thereafter as his social headquarters whenever he was in the city. But closer to his heart, partly because he helped to found it, partly because of the individuals concerned, was the Authors' Club, which held its initial meeting on October 21, 1882, in Richard Watson Gilder's "transmogrified" stable.[36] By its tenth anniversary, Eggleston as chairman for the year (the club had no president) could justifiably claim for the club a large share in raising the dignity of literature as a profession and in giving an impetus to American writing.[37] As member or guest, sooner or later practically every American writer of substance took part in meetings, though some, like Henry James, attended but seldom.

Eggleston's share in founding the American Historical Association in 1884 reflected the same firm belief that people engaged in comparable activities could benefit by professional contacts; the Association, meeting annually in different cities, necessarily had a character quite different from that of the Authors' Club. More important than either, and part of the durable bedrock of Eggleston's achievement, was the Copyright League, which he not only helped to found but served so devotedly that it seriously reduced his output of social history. In the long view this is not something to regret, however, for other men have amply extended the range of social history; but every writer, of whatever kind of book, has been the beneficiary of the international copyright act that Eggleston did so much to foster. On balance, the copyright effort was not a waste of time that might have been better spent on something else.

The fight for equitable copyright protection makes an exciting story, and a long one, for it began many years before Eggleston was born. What dragged it out was its sporadic quality; groups that authors formed for their own benefit lost their momentum and determination—lost heart, in fact, when their best efforts seemed futile. The principle of organizing for effective action was firmly recognized; what was needed was a well-organized group that would not disintegrate but would keep fighting until it won, and a nucleus, perhaps a single individual, who would be willing to make whatever sacrifices of personal ambition might prove necessary. The Authors' Club was not founded with this purpose in mind, but copyright was so often a topic of discussion that it almost seemed so. Eggleston and two other members conceived at one meeting the notion of forming an American Copyright League, specifically and exclusively devoted to winning international copyright protection.

The League soon outgrew the Club's quasi-parental support; by 1885 it had about seven hundred members. But the effective nucleus continued to be Authors' Club men; and at every point Eggleston was a key figure—never the president, who had to be some such beloved public figure as James Russell Lowell—but chairman of the executive committee, or chief lobbyist in Washington, or both at once. He participated in the "Authors' Readings," which were both popular and productive of needed funds for continuing the campaign; but more of his work was in the background: conferring with Democrats who suspected a Republican plot and with individual Republican supporters who needed constant prodding, or making arrangements for more Authors' Readings, or soliciting support from printers and typesetters, or planning receptions. "I have cranky authors to pull into line and crankier publishers to contend with. I am all at once a politician."[38]

He had mixed feelings about it: "I *am* a public-spirited man else I should never meddle with anything so little to my taste as law-making."[39] On his sixth trip to Washington within four months, he spent "an exhausting day of interviews with Senators whose notions of literary property are quite aboriginal." It gave him a certain heady satisfaction to have the League put everything in his hands. "This active leadership of a great movement is not unpleasant to my vanity & this discovery of unsuspected ability in a new direction is very gratifying. But I dreadfully grudge the time it takes and the loss it entails in many ways."[40] He refused to accept the pay that the League offered, fearing it would tie him too much to the project; but his sense of duty was an even stronger tie. He kept on doggedly, giving no public sign of the physical and mental fatigue that he spoke of only in letters to his family.

More than once victory seemed to be won, only to slip away when some Congressman hit upon a new objection and insisted on having it debated. The chief opponent was Judge Payson, an Illinois Representative, who kept reminding his colleagues that effective copyright would raise the price of books and thus harm the average reader. It was a hard argument to answer. Moncure Conway's stamp plan was also dangerous, chiefly because it split the solid front of the copyright proponents. Eggleston sent him a long, patient letter trying to reduce his intransigence: "We shall never have a literature worthy of the name," he wrote, "until the American author is protected from pirated wares. . . . Dear Mr. Conway, don't fight us if you can help it."[41]

On December 3, 1890—at the very opening of that year's short session—the Copyright Bill passed the House by a majority of forty-four; and Eggleston wrote to Lillie: "Ah if your mama could only have lived to see this victory in the House which

she looked for so long and eagerly."[42] All that year he had
suspended other activities whenever a call came from Washington. For one thing, the important Judiciary Committee of
the House would listen only to him on the subject of copyright.[43] The December triumph was premature, however, for
House and Senate differences had to be ironed out. Not until
after midnight on the final day of the session (March 3, 1891)
was the bill finally passed by the Senate and then taken to the
House. Payson, fast asleep with a newspaper over his face,
missed his final chance to object; but, even after both presiding officers had signed the bill, a Florida Senator asked for
reconsideration, which was voted down the next morning just
two hours before the session closed. President Harrison signed
the bill, most often called the Chace Act, and it went into effect
on July 1, 1891.[44] Eggleston missed this dramatic conclusion; he
had not been well since his wife's death, and he and his daughter
Allegra went to Ireland early in February, 1891. His central
contribution was recognized by the assignment of "Number 1"
under the new act, on July 1, to *The Faith Doctor*.

## IV  *Bedrock of Fame*

Pioneering in Midwestern realism and a comparable pioneering in social history are the most conspicuous veins in the bedrock of Eggleston's present reputation; whether the part he
played in copyright should be equally recognized is at least
arguable. Much that Eggleston said and wrote was of value only
to his contemporaries and is irrecoverable from the secret hearts
of men and women who responded to his ideas by being en-
lightened, solaced, emboldened, amused. The letters a few of
these people wrote and the published remininscences are a
sampling of the great affection he inspired, less by conscious
intent than by the outflow of his personality. Through his
history, he helped broaden the awareness of what America was
in the colonial past, and through his articles and stories of what
it was in the nineteenth century. His search for expression, a
dominant compulsion, contributed to other Americans' search
for self-expression.

He was one kind of American—not the only recognizable
variant of the species, but in many ways possessing what we
accept as distinctive qualities of national behavior: mobility,

restlessness, discontent with achievement to date, diversity, pragmatism, dynamism, optimism. He shared the general faith in the future, but without being indifferent to the past. He departed most from the "typical" in lacking acquisitiveness; he resorted to money-making when he had to, but most of the time he was too busy to make money. More than most citizens, he turned his saturation in varied experience to good account in his writing and speaking; but he did so more for others' benefit than for his own. He was able to overcome more physical drawbacks than most people have to cope with; despite occasional grumbling, and once he had overthrown the incubus of his early religiosity, he was a reasonably happy and optimistic man, enjoying what he wanted of the good life, and satisfied, at the end, with the degree of success he had been able to reach. He would have good reason, today, to be gratified by contemporary opinion; the erosion of fame that all men must expect has only revealed the indestructible nature of Eggleston's contribution.

# Notes and References

Letters not otherwise located in these citations are among the Eggleston Papers deposited by the Eggleston heirs in the Collection of Regional History at Cornell University.

## Chapter One

1. In *The Art of Authorship,* ed. George Bainton (London and New York, 1890), p. 277.

2. Jennie's book is named in Effa Morrison Danner, "Edward Eggleston," *Indiana Magazine of History,* XXXIII (Dec., 1937), 435-53. A careful search has not revealed that Joe's book was ever published.

3. Danner.

4. Eggleston, "Formative Influences," *The Forum,* X (Nov., 1890), 279-90.

5. R. S. Cotterill, *The Old South* (Glendale [Calif.], 1936); Ulrich B. Phillips, *Life and Labor in the Old South* (Boston, 1927).

6. Leander Monks, *Courts and Lawyers of Indiana* (Indianapolis, 1916), I, 65.

7. Clarence D. Stevens, biographical sketch of Eggleston, undated newspaper clipping.

8. Danner.

9. *Switzerland Monitor* (Vevay), May 29, 1833.

10. Schenck Papers, cited in Danner.

11. Carter, "Pioneer Lawyers," cited in Danner.

12. Eggleston, "My History," part of MS Journal (See entry for Logan, Bibliography, III, 1), and "Formative Influences."
Influences."

13. "At the Big Orchard Farm," undated clipping from *Village Times* (Vevay) cited in Danner.

14. Stevens.

15. "Formative Influences."

16. "Edward Eggleston: An Interview," *The Outlook,* LV (Feb. 6, 1897), 431-37.

17. "Formative Influences."

18. *Ibid.*

19. The daughter of one of the founders of Marietta, Ohio, where she was born in 1794, Mrs. Dumont wrote *Sketches, from Common Paths* (1856) and considerable poetry that remains uncollected. She moved to Vevay in 1814, and died in 1857. Eggles-

ton wrote a biographical sketch of her that is incorporated in May Louise Shipp's *Ohio Valley Pioneer* (unpublished).

20. Eggleston, "Books that Have Helped Me," *The Forum,* III (Aug., 1887), 49-57. This article is the central source of information about Eggleston's early reading.

21. *The Art of Authorship.*

22. "Formative Influences." Recorded also in George Cary Eggleston, *The First of the Hoosiers* (Philadephia, 1903).

23. Thomas Goodwin, "Edward Eggleston as a Boy," unlocated article cited in Danner.

24. "Books that Have Helped Me."

25. "Formative Influences."

26. "Edward Eggleston: An Interview," *The Outlook.*

27. Quoted in Danner.

28. Undated clipping from *Indiana Reveille* (Vevay), in Danner.

29. Earle E. Martin, "In His Hoosier Home," *Chicago Tribune,* July 30, 1893.

30. Martin.

31. "Formative Influences."

32. Danner.

33. "Formative Influences."

34. William Shaw to Eggleston, Nov. 16, 1852.

35. Williamson Terrell, in Madison, to Eggleston, in Vevay, Sept. 3, 1852; mother to Eggleston, Oct. 12, 1852; Terrell, in Vevay, to Eggleston, June 2, 1853.

36. P. Hamilton Baskerville, *Andrew Meade of Ireland and Virginia* (Richmond, 1921), Chap. X, "The Eggleston Family."

37. *Statistical Gazeteer of the State of Virginia . . . to 1854,* ed. Richard Edwards (Richmond, 1855).

38. MS Journal. See entry for Logan, Bibliography, III, 1.

39. Phillips, *Life and Labor in the Old South,* p. 365.

40. MS Journal.

41. "Books that Have Helped Me."

42. "Formative Influences."

43. "George Cary Eggleston," in *American Authors 1600-1900,* ed. Stanley J. Kunitz and Howard Haycraft (New York, 1938), p. 246.

44. Livia Appel and Theodore Blegen, "Official Encouragement of Immigration to Minnesota During the Territorial Period," *Minnesota History Bulletin,* V (Aug., 1923), 167-203.

45. "Address of the Managers," an American Bible Society pamphlet, 1856.

46. "My History," a section of the MS Journal.

47. "Edward Eggleston: An Interview," *The Outlook.*

48. "Formative Influences."

49. Mother to Eggleston, May 28; George to Eggleston, June 5; Jennie to Eggleston, June 6; Terrell to Eggleston, June 17—all in 1856.

50. Notebook 1, part of MS Journal, list of sermons delivered.

51. E. E. Long to Eggleston, June 9, 1856.

52. F. W. Frink, *A Short History of Faribault* (Faribault, 1901), and Franklyn Curtiss-Wedge, *History of Rice and Steele Counties, Minnesota* (Chicago, 1910).

53. Eggleston to his mother, July 30, 1856.

54. Martin, "In His Hoosier Home."

55. Eggleston preseerved this certificate along with other papers at his Lake George home.

56. William Shaw to Eggleston, April 1, 1856.

57. G. C. Smith, Moonshill, Indiana, to Eggleston, Oct. 11, 1856.

58. R. M. Barnes, "Personal Recollections of the Late Edward Eggleston," unlocated newspaper clipping.

59. "My History," part of MS Journal.

60. Notebook 1, list of sermons.

61. Barnes.

62. Notebook 1 gives the preaching stations as Bellview, Salt Fork, Sugar Grove, Wesley Chapel, Union, Yorkville, Guilford, Olive Branch, Sandon's, and Logan Corners.

63. Barnes.

64. Part of MS Journal.

65. Notebook 1.

## Chapter Two

1. Notebook 1; William McKinley, *A Story of Minnesota Methodism* (Cincinnati, 1911), Chap. XIV, "Edward Eggleston," pp. 65-70.

2. Terrell to Eggleston, June 8, 1857.

3. *Ibid.*, June 15, 1857.

4. "Journal for A.D. 1858," part of MS Journal.

5. Terrell to Eggleston, July 15, 1857.

6. A certificate of his Indiana record had been mailed on June 1, according to G. C. Smith to Eggleston, June 1, 1857, and Terrell to Eggleston, June 8, 1857.

7. *Minutes of the Minnesota Annual Conference of the Methodist Episcopal Church* (hereafter called *Conference Minutes*), for 1857.

8. George Cary Eggleston to Eggleston, July 25, 1857.

9. *Ibid.*, Sept. 1, 1857.

10. Terrell to Eggleston, July 17, Sept. 10, 1857.

11. George to Eggleston, Oct. 26, 1858.

12. Notebook 1.

13. Randel, "Edward Eggleston's Library at Traverse des Sioux," *Minnesota History*, XXVI (Sept., 1945), 242-47.

*Notes and References*

14. Unlocated newspaper clipping, Winona, about 1865.
15. MS Journal, Jan. 7, 8, 10, 1858.
16. Terrell to Eggleston, Sept. 10, 1857.
17. Jennie to Eggleston, Oct. 16, 1857.
18. Bettie Cocke to Eggleston, Nov. 4, 1857.
19. "Strong typhoid symptoms," MS Journal, March 31, 1858.
20. MS Journal, Jan. 17, 1858.
21. MS Journal, March 19, 1858.
22. McKinley, *A Story of Minnesota Methodism.*
23. *Conference Minutes* for 1858.
24. Eggleston to Lizzie, April 16, 1858.
25. Notebook 1.
26. Eggleston to Lizzie, June 27, 1858.
27. *Ibid.,* July 21, 1858.
28. *Ibid.,* July 26, 1858.
29. Terrell to Eggleston, Sept. 30, 1858.
30. Chaffee to Eggleston, Nov. 2, 1858.
31. *American Bible Society, 43rd Report,* 1859, p. 88.
32. *Records of Quarterly Conference of Market St. Station, Methodist Episcopal Church, Minnesota Conf.,* 1858.
33. *Conference Minutes* for 1859.
34. *Records of Quarterly Conference,* 1858.
35. MS Journal, Aug. 30, Sept. 2, 3, 1859.
36. MS Journal, Sept. 22, 30, 1859.
37. MS Journal, Oct. 4, 1859.
38. MS Journal, Nov. 16, 1859.
39. MS Journal, Sept. 24, 1859.
40. *Conference Minutes* for 1859 and 1860.
41. *Minnesotian and Times* (St. Paul), June 21, July 6, 11, 18, 1860. Scudder subsequently published his own account of the expedition in *The Winnipeg Country, or Roughing It with an Eclipse Party* (Boston, 1886).
42. *Minnesotian and Times,* March 6, 1860.
43. XX (Dec., 1860), 726-29.
44. Reviewed by Eggleston in *The Independent,* Dec. 8, 1870.
45. XX (Nov., 1859), 667.
46. MS Journal, April 30, 1860.
47. "Books that Have Helped Me."
48. MS Journal, Sept. 27, 1860.
49. MS Journal, Sept. 17, 1860.
50. Joseph to Eggleston, Dec. 24, 1860.
51. Minor T. Thomas, Fort Snelling, to Eggleston, May 19, 1861.
52. N. H. Babcock, Jr., New York, to Eggleston, Dec. 22, 1861; Nichols & Dean, St. Paul, to Eggleston, various dates, 1861.

53. Advertisement in Mankato *Semi-Weekly Record,* Jan. 4—May 31, 1862.

54. A. D. Cunningham, Mooresville, Ind., to Eggleston, May 19, 1861.

55. Eggleston to Lizzie, May 6, 1862; St. Paul *Daily Press,* May 10, 1862.

56. E. D. Neill, *History of Ramsey County* (Minneapolis, 1881).

57. W. R. Marshall, in camp at Lower Sioux Agency, to Eggleston, Oct. 27, 1862.

58. Eggleston's first Indian story, "An Incident of the Indian Massacres of 1862," appeared in *The Ladies' Repository* in December, 1864; all the other Indian stories were in *The Little Corporal,* August 1865 to December 1866.

59. *The Ladies Repository,* XXIV (Jan., 1864), 20-22.

60. *Conference Minutes* for 1859, 1863.

61. St. Paul *Daily Press,* Aug. 24, 1864.

62. Terrell to Eggleston, June 29, 1863.

63. E. B. and E. C. Treat, Chicago, to Eggleston, July 8, 1863.

64. C. H. Kellogg, Kenosha, to Eggleston, July 31, Aug. 5, 7, 17, 21, 28, 1863; Walter L. Griffith, New York, to Eggleston, numerous dates from Aug. 19 to Dec. 30, 1863.

65. Hurlburt, Williams & Co., Hartford, to Eggleston, June 30, 1863.

66. Eggleston to Lizzie, July 6, 1863.

67. The Sioux Outbreak still awaits its adequate historian.

68. Neill, *History of Ramsey County,* pp. 400, 426.

69. Eggleston to Thomas Simpson, April 10, 1863. Owned by Minnesota Historical Society.

70. Eggleston to Lizzie, April 25, 1863.

71. Eggleston to E. and H. Anthony, Feb. 8, 1864.

72. Eggleston to Lizzie, Feb. 24, March 8, 1864.

73. *Ibid.,* April 2, 1864.

74. *Ibid.,* April 26, 1864.

75. *Ibid.,* April 22, 1864.

76. Simpson to Eggleston, Aug. 29, 1864.

77. Eggleston to Lizzie, Sept. 23, 1864.

78. *Conference Minutes* for 1864.

79. Eggleston to Lizzie, Sept. 29, 1864.

80. *History of Methodism in Minnesota* (Red Wing, 1887), p. 193.

81. *Harper's* to Eggleston, June 18, 1864.

82. Bettie Cocke to Eggleston, Sept. 8, 1864.

83. Mrs. Simpson to Eggleston, July 15, 1864.

84. *Voices of the Fair* (Chicago, 1864).

85. Bentley to Eggleston, Dec. 15, 1864.

86. *Northwest Sanitary Fair* (St. Paul, 1865), three-page pamphlet signed by Eggleston and Gov. Stephen Miller.

87. William Goodsmith to Lizzie, Feb. 14, 1865.

88. Franklin William Scott, *Newspapers and Periodicals of Illinois* (Springfield, 1910), p. 83.

89. Sewell to Eggleston, Nov. 4, 9, 1865.

90. *Ibid.*, Dec. 14, 1865.

91. *Ibid.*, Dec. 2, 1865.

92. *Ibid.*, Jan. 12, 1866.

93. *Ibid.*, Feb. 8(?), 1866.

94. Terrell to Eggleston, Jan. 13, 1866.

95. C. Brooks to Eggleston, Jan. 22, 1864.

96. Sewell to Eggleston, March 12, 1866.

97. Marshall to Eggleston, April 27, 1866.

98. *The Little Corporal,* II (June, 1866), 94.

99. *Conference Minutes* for 1866.

## Chapter Three

1. Eggleston to Lizzie, Dec. 12, 1866.

2. St. Paul *Press,* Dec. 20, 1866.

3. Sept. 14, Oct. 4, 23, 1866.

4. Editor of *Harper's* to Eggleston, Oct. 24, 1866.

5. Ticknor & Fields to Eggleston, Nov. 7, 1866.

6. Editor of *Harper's* to Eggleston, April 26, 1867.

7. *Harper's New Monthly Magazine,* LXXXVIII (Feb., 1894), 466-75.

8. Editor of *Harper's* to Eggleston, Nov. 11, 1866.

9. "Little Crow, the Sioux Chief," *The Little Corporal,* I (Dec., 1865), 51-52.

10. *The Ladies' Repository,* XXVI (July, 1866), 388-94.

11. *The Little Corporal,* IV (Jan., 1867), 10-11.

12. Stephen Paine, *A Critical Study of the Novels of Edward Eggleston* (Ann Arbor: University Microfilms, 1962), p. 238.

13. *Ibid.*, p. 237 *passim.*

14. The first "Feuilleton" appeared on Nov. 17, 1866, the last on Sept. 28, 1867.

15. Note in *The Little Corporal,* IV (March, 1867), 45.

16. Eggleston to Lizzie, March 18, 1867.

17. *Ibid.*, March 22, 1867.

18. Minutes of Depauw chapter of Phi Gamma Delta for March 22, 1867.

19. Eggleston to Lizzie, March 28, 30, 1867.

20. "Prisons and Poor-Houses," Chicago *Tribune,* June 13, 1867.

21. Philip G. Gilette to Eggleston, June 14, 1867.

22. "Prisons and Poor-Houses," Chicago *Tribune,* Oct. 30, 1867.

23. Eggleston to Lizzie, various dates in Nov. and Dec., 1867.

24. *Ibid.*, April ?, 1869.

25. *Ibid.*, various letters, Sept. 12-19, 1867.

26. The name of this periodical had been changed at the beginning of the year 1869 by the addition of the word *National.*

27. A review printed before the fire—in *Scribner's Monthly,* II (June, 1871), 221—is evidence that at least one pre-publication copy was issued.

28. The dedication reads as follows:

TO OUR

LITTLE SILVERHAIR

Who used to listen to My Stories;

BUT WHO IS NOW

Listening to the Christmas Stories of the Angels,

THIS BOOK IS DEDICATED.

29. "Book Table," *The Independent,* Oct. 6, 1870.

30. "Books for Boys," Jan. 12, 1871.

31. "Book Table," Sept. 1, 1870.

32. "Book Table," Nov. 3, 1870.

33. "Book Table," Feb. 2, 1871.

34. "Book Table," Nov. 24, 1870.

35. "Book Table," Oct. 6, 1870.

36. "The Westminster Review on American Literature," Nov. 17, 1870.

37. Under "Two Victories of Statesmanship," July 6, 1871.

38. Eggleston to Lillie, Feb. 21, 1888.

39. W. H. Ward, "Sixty Years of the Independent," *The Independent,* Dec. 10, 1908.

40. The letters from Longfellow and Lowell are among a collection owned by the Eggleston heirs.

41. Alice Cary to Eggleston, [?] 1871. Alice and her sister Phoebe both died in this year, 1871.

42. Bryant to Eggleston, Jan. [?], 1871. The excerpt he sent was printed in *The Independent* on Feb. 2, 1871, with the title "The Palace and Gardens of Alcinous." The completed *Odyssey* was published 1871-72.

43. "Charles Sumner's Removal," *The Independent,* March 16, 1871.

44. Howells to Eggleston, Jan. 21, 1871. Owned by Eggleston heirs.

45. George Cary Eggleston, Chapters XV and XVII of *The First of the Hoosiers.*

46. "The Disappearance of Tweed," *Hearth and Home,* Jan. 13, 1872.

## Chapter Four

1. Eggleston gave December 15, 1871, as the publication date in a copy he inscribed for Hamlin Garland, who reproduced the inscription in his *Roadside Meetings* (New York, 1930), p. 359.

2. "Formative Influences," *The Forum*, X (Nov., 1890), 290.

3. Under "Periodicals," Dec. 8, 1870.

4. Cowie, *The Rise of the American Novel* (New York, 1948), p. 833.

5. Comment in obituary notice, Brooklyn *Eagle*, Sept. 4, 1902.

6. Original in Eggleston Papers; reprinted in Randel, "Edward Eggleston on Dialect," *American Speech*, XXX (May, 1955), 111-14.

7. By James A. Harrison, in *Anglia*, VII (1884), 232-79.

8. *Century Magazine*, XLVII (April, 1894), 848-56; and XLVIII (Oct., 1894), 867-75.

9. *Scribner's Monthly*, V (Dec., 1872), 270.

10. *Ibid.*, VI (Sept., 1873), 563.

11. Review by J. R. Dennett, *The Nation*, XIV (Jan. 18, 1872), 44-46.

12. *The Nation*, XVI (June 12, 1873), 404.

13. *Appleton's Journal*, IX (May 3, 1873), 605.

14. *The Christian Union*, VII (June 4, 1873), 443-44.

15. *The Nation*, XIX (Sept. 24, 1874), 207.

16. *Lippincott's Magazine of Popular Literature and Science*, XIII (June, 1874), 776.

17. *The Atlantic Monthly*, XXXIII (June, 1874), 745-47.

18. *Scribner's Monthly*, XIX (July, 1874), 374-75.

19. John T. Flanagan, "The Novels of Edward Eggleston," *College English*, V (Feb., 1944), 250-54.

20. "Unconsidered Trifles of Southern Travel," *Hearth and Home*, May 17, 1873.

21. "Sleeping on a Mountain-Top," *Hearth and Home*, Sept. 20, 1873.

22. "To the Saguenay Headlands," *The Christian Union*, Sept. 16, 1874.

23. "Edward Eggleston, D. D.," LXI (Dec., 1875), 376-79.

24. Eggleston to editor, Brooklyn *Daily Times*, July 20, 1876.

25. Interview, "Novel Church Enterprise," New York *Tribune*, Dec. 27, 1876.

26. Eggleston to James H. Smart, March 15, 1876. Owned by Indiana Historical Society.

27. Eggleston to Howells, June 17, 1875. Owned by Harvard College Library.

28. Brooklyn *Daily Times*, June 23, 25, 1877.

29. Mary M. Eggleston, Granville, Ohio (a distant cousin), to author, June, 1941, recalling Eggleston's lecture there on Feb. 29, 1892.

30. Eggleston to his family, July 16, 19, 21, 1877.

31. "Sights Abroad," July 10; "Trifles of Travel," July 31; "Glimpses of Travel," Aug. 10.

32. Eggleston to Lizzie, July 23, 1877.

33. *Ibid.*, July 29, 1877.

34. *Ibid.*, July 30, Aug. 2, 5, 10, 1877.

35. *Owl's Nest Family Book*, property of Eggleston heirs.

36. Holland to Eggleston, June 7, 1877.

37. An unlocated article ("Edward Eggleston, Preacher, Editor, and Novelist") estimated that up to 1877 *The Hoosier School-Master* had sold 45,000 copies; *The End of the World*, 25,000; *The Mystery of Metropolisville*, 14,000; and *The Circuit Rider*, 25,000.

38. *The Atlantic Monthly*, XLIII (April, 1879), 504-6.

39. *The Nation*, XXVII (Oct. 17, 1878), 244.

40. *Scribner's Monthly*, XVII (Dec., 1878), 302-3.

41. *Harper's New Monthly Magazine*, LVIII (Dec., 1878), 146.

42. *Vanity Fair*, XX (Sept. 28, 1878), 175.

43. Eggleston to daughter Blanche, March 27, 1879.

44. Parallels pointed out by Paine.

45. Eggleston to Lizzie, Oct. 7, 1883.

46. Introduction to *The Hoosier School-Boy* (New York, 1936), p. vii.

47. Eggleston to Lillie, Jan. 10, 1886.

48. Eggleston to Allegra, March 25, 1890.

49. Preface to *The Faith Doctor* (New York, 1891), p. 4.

## Chapter Five

1. Notebook 1.

2. Eggleston to Lillie, Jan. 28, 1878.

3. *Ibid.*, April 7, 1878.

4. *Ibid.*, Dec. 29, 1878.

5. *Ibid.*, Jan. 10, 1879.

6. *Ibid.*, Jan. 22, 1879.

7. "Parsons and Parsons," *The Christian Union*, XVII (Nov., 1878), 139-46, and (Feb., 1879), 483-90.

8. Eggleston to Lillie, Feb. 10, 1879.

9. *Ibid.*, Oct. 2, 1879; McKinley, *A Story of Minnesota Methodism*, p. 119.

10. Eggleston to Lillie, Nov. 6, 1879.

11. "Edward Eggleston: An Interview."

12. Eggleston to Lizzie, Feb. 9, 1882.
13. Eggleston to Lillie, Feb. 17, 1881.
14. Eggleston to Lizzie, Feb. 9, 1882.
15. Eggleston to Lillie, March 18, 1883.
16. Eggleston to Allegra, Feb. 14, 1881.
17. Eggleston to Lillie, Feb. 3, 1881.
18. Eggleston to Lizzie, Feb. 14, 1883.
19. Eggleston to Lillie, March 30, 1883.
20. Eggleston to Lizzie, Feb. 11, 1883.
21. Eggleston to Lillie, Jan. 30, Feb. 16-17, March 9, May ?, June 13-14, 22, July 5, 1880.
22. *Ibid.*, July 21, 1880.
23. *Ibid.*, Aug. 31, 1880.
24. Eggleston's history collection, acquired by the New York State Library, was accessioned between 1912 and 1934. The numbering goes from 1 to 3576, with some blanks reducing the actual total.
25. Eggleston to Allegra, April 6, 13, 1890.
26. Eggleston to Lillie, May 18, 1902.
27. "Edward Eggleston: An Interview."
28. Eggleston to Lillie, June 14, 1880.
29. Jane Zimmerman to Eggleston, Dec. 6, 1896.
30. Joseph to Frances, Jan. 2, 1897.
31. "A Reception to Dr. Eggleston," *The Critic*, XXIX (Dec. 12, 1896), 389-90.
32. *Annual Report of the American Historical Association for 1890*, p. 7.
33. "Cavalier and Puritan," Brooklyn *Eagle*, Jan. 10, 1897.
34. Brooklyn *Life*, Nov. 28, 1896.
35. Philadephia *Press*, Dec. 27, 1896.
36. Jan. 2 (or 3), 1897.
37. Baltimore *Sun*, Jan. 23, 1897.
38. San Francisco *Report*, Jan. 23, 1897.
39. Brooklyn *Citizen*, Dec. 13, 1896.
40. New York *Mail and Express*, April 24, 1897.
41. *The Critic*, Jan. 2, 1897.
42. *The Congregationalist*, March 11, 1897.
43. *The Book Buyer*, April, 1897.
44. *The Independent*, XLIV (Jan. 21, 1897), 89.
45. "Dr. Eggleston on American Origins," *The Forum*, XXII (Nov., 1896), 590-99.
46. Rochester *Post-Express*, Jan. 2, 1897.
47. Watertown *Daily Standard*, Nov. 25, 1896.
48. Eggleston to Lillie, Jan. 9, 1899.
49. *American Historical Review*, VI (July, 1901), 802-5.
50. XVII (March, 1902), 162-66.

51. *A Bibliography of History for Schools and Libraries,* ed. C. M. Andrews, J. Montgomery Gambrill, and Lila Lee Tall (New York, 1911), p. 103.

52. *A History of American History* (New York, 1937), pp. 388-89.

53. V, 440-41.

## Chapter Six

1. Eggleston to Lillie, April 17, 1898.

2. Eggleston to Herbert B. Adams, April 14, 1898, in *Historical Scholarship in the United States, 1876-1901; as Revealed in the Correspondence of Herbert B. Adams,* ed. W. Stull Holt (Baltimore, 1904), pp. 253-54.

3. Charles Hirschfeld, "Edward Eggleston: Pioneer in Social History," *Historiography and Urbanization: Essays in Honor of W. Stull Holt,* ed. Eric F. Goldman (Baltimore, 1941), p. 209.

4. Eggleston to Lillie, Feb. 22, 1891.

5. Eggleston to President Cleveland, Feb. 22, 1891. Owned by Library of Congress.

6. Eggleston to President McKinley, Aug. 2, 1898. Owned by Library of Congress. Reply: J. A. Porter to Eggleston, Aug. 5, 1898.

7. Eggleston to Lillie, Dec. 1897; Garland, *A Daughter of the Middle Border* (New York, 1921), pp. 55-56.

8. George Cary Eggleston to Eggleston, Jan. 1, 1899.

9. Nicholson to Eggleston, Jan. 5, Feb. 14, March 9, 26, 1900.

10. Rule to Eggleston, Oct. 18, Dec. 12, 1901.

11. E. Ballou to Eggleston, Nov. 10, 1901.

12. Lowes to Eggleston, Feb. 12, March 28, 1900; Oct. 22, 1900 or 1901; Lowes to Frances, Feb. 12, 1900; Jan. 7, 1903.

13. Eggleston to Lizzie, Dec. ?, 1883.

14. Eggleston to Lillie, Jan. 1, June 24, 1885.

15. *Ibid.,* April 16, 1891.

16. Eggleston to Brander Matthews, August ?, 1885. Owned by Columbia University Library.

17. Eggleston to Lizzie, July 21, 1877.

18. *Ibid.,* Sept. 30, 1887; "Stevensonia," *The Critic,* XXVI (Jan. 21, 1895), 31.

19. Perry, *And Gladly Teach* (Boston, 1935), p. 140; Perry to author, Oct. 25, 1943.

20. Tarkington to author, April 5, 1940; Garland, *My Friendly Contemporaries* (New York, 1923), p. 131.

21. *Outlook* interview, 1897.

22. Robinson to Eggleston, Feb. 9, 1897. Owned by Eggleston heirs.

23. Hirschfeld, p. 209.

24. Eggleston to Lillie, Nov. 20, 1881.

25. *Ibid.*, Feb. 4 and 5, 1882.

26. Eggleston to Matthews, June 23, Aug. 6, 10, 13, 20 (?), 1885. Owned by Columbia University Library. E. C. Stedman to Eggleston, July 4, 1885. Owned by Eggleston heirs.

27. Appleton to Eggleston, Oct. 16; Hutton to Eggleston, Nov. 11; Putnam to Eggleston, Nov. 19; Gilder to Eggleston, Nov. 12; Straus to Eggleston, Nov. 7, 11, 16, 1896, and April 27, 1897. Owned by Eggleston heirs.

28. Kresel to Eggleston, Aug. 8, Oct. 24, Nov. 15, 16, 1893.

29. Eggleston to Lillie, Nov. 26, 1893.

30. Kresel to Eggleston, Dec. 13, 1893.

31. Straus to Eggleston, Dec. 20, 1901. Kresel subsequently became a successful attorney in New York; he served as counsel for the Seabury investigation. He died in 1957.

32. "In Memoriam—Emma Lazarus," *The American Hebrew*, XXX (Dec. 9, 1887), 69.

33. "Dr. Holland the Moralist," *The Christian Union*, XII (Oct., 13, 1875), 297-98.

34. Eggleston to Allegra, Aug. 23, 1893.

35. "Books that Have Helped Me."

36. Matthews, *These Many Years* (New York, 1917), pp. 220, 224.

37. "From Writing to Speaking," New York *Tribune*, March 1, 1893; "The Authors' Decennial Dinner," *The Critic*, XXII (March 4, 1893), 131-35.

38. Eggleston to Lillie, Jan. 7, 1888.

39. *Ibid.*, Feb. 21, 1888.

40. *Ibid.*, April 29, 1888.

41. Eggleston to Conway, Jan. 17, 1888. Owned by Columbia University Library.

42. Eggleston to Lillie, Dec. 5, 1890.

43. *Ibid.*, Jan. 12, 1890.

44. Robert U. Johnson, "How International Copyright Was Won," *Remembered Yesterdays* (Boston, 1923), pp. 241-61; George H. Putnam, *The Copyright Question* (New York, 1890), pp. 56-63.

# Selected Bibliography

PRIMARY SOURCES

The Eggleston Papers, deposited by the Eggleston heirs in the Collection of Regional History at Cornell University, include virtually all the letters written by Eggleston to members of his family, and their letters to him, together with the bulk of the surviving letters written to Eggleston by other individuals. The manuscripts of all his novels except *The Hoosier School-Master* are included, as are the manuscripts of many of his stories, articles, and poems; several of his notebooks; about 125 sermons and sixty-nine fragments of sermons; notes on dialect; several thousand notes for his histories; notes for books never completed (e. g., *The Winter Evening Book, Tell Me a Story,* and *Agnostic*). Notebook 1 lists early sermons and books owned; another notebook contains notes made while writing *The Mystery of Metropolisville, The Circuit Rider,* and several articles. Scrapbooks contain his contributions to the Chicago *Evening Journal, The Independent, Hearth and Home,* and other periodicals. There are also reviews; maps and passports; newspaper clippings; publishers' accounts; obituaries; and other papers. Retained by the Eggleston heirs is a collection of letters written to Eggleston by various eminent individuals, together with such private memorabilia as the *Owl's Nest Family Book*.

Most of the letters and manuscripts held by libraries in the United States are conveniently listed in *American Literary Manuscripts* (Austin: University of Texas Press, 1960), p. 115. In addition, the following libraries are known to have some original Eggleston material: American Antiquarian Society, Evanston Historical Society, Iowa State Department of History and Archives, Library of Congress, Minnesota Historical Society, and Northwestern University Library. The Bodleian Library at Oxford has three Eggleston letters in its Bryce Papers. Eggleston was so prolific a letter-writer that additional letters find their way into library collections each year.

I. *Books*

Sunday school books:

Sunday-School Conventions and Institutes, with Suggestions on County and Township Organization. Chicago: Adams, Blackmer, & Lyon, 1867. No copy located. Advertised in *The Manual* (1869). Library of Congress owns a copy of the second edition, 1870.

*Improved Sunday-School Record*. Chicago: Adams, Blackmer & Lyon, 1869. No copy located. Listed in James Kelly, *The American Catalogue*, Vol. II.

*The Manual: A Practical Guide to the Sunday-School Work*. Chicago: Adams, Blackmer, and Lyon, 1869. Reprinted in 1870 and 1872.

*Tracts for Sunday School Teachers*. Chicago: Adams, Blackmer, & Lyon, n.d. (but in period 1870-72). Cover title: *Counsel for Teachers*.

*Mr. Blake's Walking-Stick*. Chicago: Adams, Blackmer & Lyon; New York: A. D. F. Randolph & Co., 1870. This is Eggleston's longest short story, virually a novelette. Reprinted 1872.

*Book of Queer Stories and Stories Told on a Cellar Door*. Chicago: Adams, Blackmer, and Lyon, 1871. Destroyed, plates and all, in the Chicago Fire of 1871. Reviewed in *Scribner's Monthly*, II (June, 1871), 221.

*The Hoosier School-Master. A Novel*. New York: Orange Judd and Company, 1871. Serialized in *Hearth and Home*, Sept. 30– Dec. 30, 1871. Numerous reprintings, including New Uniform Edition (New York: Charles Scribner's Sons, 1881); Library Edition, revised, with an introduction and notes on the dialect (New York: Orange Judd, 1892); Modern Readers' Series, introduction by Emory Holloway (New York: Macmillan, 1928).

*The End of the World. A Love Story*. New York: Orange Judd, 1872. Serialized in *Hearth and Home*, April 20–Sept. 7, 1872.

*The Mystery of Metropolisville*. New York: Orange Judd, 1873. Serialized in *Hearth and Home*, Dec. 7, 1872–April 26, 1873.

*The Circuit Rider. A Tale of the Heroic Age*. New York: J. B. Ford and Company, 1874. Serialized in *The Christian Union*, Nov. 13, 1873–March 18, 1874.

*The Schoolmaster's Stories for Boys and Girls*. Boston: Henry L. Shepard & Co., 1874. Twenty-five stories collected from various magazines.

*Christ in Literature*. Compiled and edited. New York: J. B. Ford and Company, 1875. Preface dated October, 1874.

*Christ in Art*. Compiled and edited. New York: J. B. Ford and Company, 1875. Preface dated November, 1874.

*Roxy*. New York: Charles Scribner's Sons, 1878. Serialized in *Scribner's Monthly*, Nov., 1877–Oct., 1878.

Series "Famous American Indians," co-author, Lillie Eggleston Seelye, published by Dodd, Mead & Company, New York: *Tecumseh and the Indian Prophet*, 1878; *Pocahontas*, 1879; *Brant and Red Jacket*, 1879; *Montezuma and the Conquest of Mexico*, 1880.

*The Hoosier School-Boy.* New York: Charles Scribner's Sons, 1883. Serialized in *St. Nicholas,* Dec., 1881–April, 1882.

*Queer Stories for Boys and Girls.* New York: Charles Scribner's Sons, 1884. A new selection of stories chosen from previous collections.

*The Graysons. A Story of Illinois.* New York: The Century Company, 1888. Serialized in *The Century Magazine,* Nov., 1887–Aug., 1888.

*A History of the United States and Its People.* New York: D. Appleton and Company, 1888. Several variants of this book appeared: one, the same year, added to the title the words *for the Use of Schools*; another, in 1889, was called *The Household History of the United States and Its People for Young Americans.*

*Why the Copyright Bill Should Pass.* n. p.: American Copyright League, 1890. A pamphlet, signed by Eggleston (as chairman) and the four other members of the League's executive committee.

*The Faith Doctor. A Story of New York.* New York: D. Appleton and Company, 1891. Serialized in *The Century Magazine,* Feb.–Oct., 1891. The first book to be issued under the new copyright law, entered with the date July 1, 1891.

*The Schoolmaster in Literature,* ed. Hubert Skinner. New York: American Book Company, 1892. Introduction by Eggleston, and two selections from his writings: an excerpt from *The Hoosier School-Master* and "Some Western Schoolmasters."

Series "The Delights of History," co-author with Lillie Eggleston Seelye, illustrated by Allegra Eggleston, published by D. Appleton and Company, New York: *The Story of Columbus,* 1892; *The Story of Washington,* 1893.

*Duffels.* New York: D. Appleton and Company, 1893. Collected short stories.

*The First Book of the Authors' Club. Liber Scriptorum.* New York: The Authors' Club, 1893. Eggleston's contribution: "In Defense of the Dead," pp. 208-13.

School readers published by American Book Company, 1895, in variant forms: *Stories of American Life and Adventure* (for third grade); *Stories of Great Americans for Little Americans* (for second grade).

*Sister Tabea.* New York: D. Appleton and Company, 1896. Reprinted from *Duffels.*

*The Beginners of a Nation. A History of the Source and Rise of the Earliest English Settlements in America with Special Reference to the Life and Character of the People.* New York: D. Appleton and Company, 1896. Reprinted, Beacon Press, 1959; intro. by A. M. Schlesinger.

Selected Bibliography

*The Transit of Civilization from England to America in the Seventeenth Century.* New York: D. Appleton and Company, 1901. Reprinted by Peter Smith, 1960; intro. by A. M. Schlesinger.

*The New Century History of the United States.* New York, Cincinnati, Chicago: American Book Company, 1904. Preface by George Cary Eggleston, dated Sept., 1903.

## II *Periodical contributions*

"Waiting for the Daybreak," *The Ladies' Repository,* XIX (Nov., 1859), 667. A poem.

"Beranger, the Poet of the People," *The Ladies' Repository,* XX (Dec., 1860), 726-29.

(Reports from an eclipse expedition). Letters to the St. Paul *Minnesotian and Times,* June 21, July 6, 11, 18, 1860.

"Christian Patriotism," Stillwater *Messenger,* May 28, 1861. Excerpts from a sermon.

"The Bible in Modern Languages," *The Ladies' Repository,* XXIV (Jan., 1864), 20-22.

"Letter to General Gorman from a Hoosier," St. Paul *Daily Press,* Aug. 24, 1864. Signed Zoroaster Higgins.

"An Incident of the Indian Massacres of 1862," *The Ladies' Repository,* XXIV (Dec., 1864), 709-11.

*Series:* "Round Table Stories" in *The Little Corporal:* "The Trapper and the Indians. A True Story," I (Aug., 1865), 17-18. "True Story of an Indian Chief," I (Sept., 1865), 37-38.

"Little Crow, the Sioux Chief," I (Oct., 1865), 51-52.

"Indian Legends," I (Nov., 1865), 65-66. "Other-Day, the Faithfull Indian," I (Dec., 1865), 81-83. "How the Indian God Made the World," II (Jan., 1866), 7-9. "The Foolish Indian. A Dacota Fireside Story," II (Feb., 1866), 25-26. "The Lazy Indian; and Other True Stories," II (March, 1866), 40-42. "Peter Peterson, the Captive Norwegian Boy," II (April, 1866), 56-58. "A May-Day Frolic, and Some Indian Legends," II (May, 1866), 72-74. "The Rocky Mountain Leap," II (June, 1866), 87-89.

"1866. New Year's Address of the Winona Republican," Winona *Daily Republican,* Jan. 1, 1866. Eleven poems of topical interest.

"The Antwerp Laborer and His Family," *The Ladies' Repository,* XXVI (July, 1866), 388–94. Translated from the French of Hendrick Conscience.

Series "Evenings at the Nest" in *The Little Corporal:* "The Legend of Mandua," III (July, 1866), 7-9. "The Indians and the Telescope," III (Aug., 1866), 27. "Mr. Spencer's Captivity," III

(Sept., 1866), 42-43. "Anecdotes of Indians," III (Dec., 1866), 85-86.

"Organized to Death," *The Sunday School Teacher*, I (Oct., 1866), 297-98.

Series "Our Saturday Feuilleton" in Chicago *Evening Journal*: "Life in the Street Cars," Nov. 17, 1866. "The Literature of Signs," Nov. 24, 1866. "Show Windows," Dec. 1, 1866. "News-boys," Jan. 26, 1867. "Sensations in Chicago," Feb. 2, 1867. "Mr. Jones and His Dinner," Feb. 9, 1867. "The Turkey that Got Pecked," Feb. 16, 1867. "The People in the Streets," Feb. 23, 1867. "The Death of the Dogs," March 9, 1867. "Handbills and Posters," March 16, 1867. "The Bridges," April 13, 1867. "Chignons and Microscopes," April 20, 1867. "Artesians," April 27, 1867. "The First of May," May 4, 1867. "Grievances," May 18, 1867. "The Servant Girl," Sept. 28, 1867. "Servant Girls and Their Mistresses," Oct. 5, 1867. "Soliloquy of a Waiter." Date unknown. "Day and Night in the Streets." Date unknown.

"Second Year with Jesus," *The Sunday School Teacher*, II (Jan.–Dec., 1867).

Editor's Table. *The Sunday School Teacher*. II (Jan.–Dec., 1867), III (Jan.–Dec., 1868), IV (Jan.–Dec., 1869). Authorship not certain, but implied from fact that Eggleston was the editor.

"The Unfortunate Widow," *The Little Corporal*, IV (Jan., 1867), 4-5. Translated from the Italian.

"Early Times in Chicago. A Story by Captain John," *The Little Corporal*, IV (Jan., 1867), 10-11.

"Prisons and Poor-Houses," Chicago *Tribune*, June 13 and Oct. 30, 1867. Signed Clef de Voute.

Supernatural stories in *The Little Corporal*: "The Wonderful Bird of Eden," IV (June, 1867), 84-85. "Simon and the Garuly," V (Aug., 1867), 20-21. "Lazy Larkin and the Joblilies," V (Sept., 1867), 36-37. "The Great Panjandrum Himself," V (Dec., 1867), 83-85.

"Western Correspondence," *The Independent*, XIX-XXI (1867-69), bi-weekly. Signed Penholder.

"A Famine and a Feast," *Our Young Folks*, III (Nov., 1867), 682-86.

"A Year with the Apostles," *The Sunday School Teacher*, III (Jan.-Dec., 1868).

Stories in *The Little Corporal*, VI (1868): "Crooked Jack," March, 43-44. "Widow Wiggins' Wonderful Cat," May, 75-76. "The Funny Little Old Woman," June, 82-83.

Articles in *The Independent*, XX, 1868: "Lay Preaching at the West," April 23; "The Methodist General Conference," May 21, June 4; "The Methodist General Conference and the Republican National Convention," May 28; "International Convention of Young Men's Christian Associations," July 2; "The Epoch of Sunday-Schools," Dec. 10.

"Studies in the Epistles," *The National Sunday School Teacher,* IV (Jan.–Sept., 1869).

"Our Western Letter," *The Independent,* Oct. 14, 1869–May 12, 1870.

Articles in *The Independent,* XXI, 1869: "Wood, Hay, Stubble," Feb. 11; "The Woman's Suffrage Convention at Chicago," Feb. 25; "The National Sunday-School Convention," May 6,

Articles in *The Independent,* XXII, 1870: "The Methodist Book Concern," May 26; "George Sand's Hermit," Oct. 6; "The Sunday School," Oct. 6; "Personal," Oct. 20: "The November Magazines," Oct. 27; "The Westminster Review on American Literature," Nov. 17; "Independent Book Criticism," Dec. 1. Articles for 1871 (until July 13) are too numerous to list separately.

Book Table. *The Independent,* XXII, 1870: Sept. 29, Oct. 13, 29, Nov. 3, 10, 24, Dec. 1, 8, 15.

"Huldah the Help. A Thanksgiving Love Story," *Scribner's Monthly,* I (Dec., 1870), 189-96. Reprinted in *Duffels.*

"Ben: A Story for May-Day," *Scribner's Monthly,* II (May, 1871), 71-77.

"The Gunpowder Plot," *Scribner's Monthly,* II (July, 1871), 252-59. A story, reprinted in *Duffels.*

"Uncle Sim's Boy," *Hearth and Home,* III, Aug. 19, 26, Sept. 2, 1871. The first experiment with a serial story.

Editorial articles in *Hearth and Home,* from Aug. 19, 1871, until Dec. 4, 1873, are too numerous to list separately; some weekly issues carry as many as six. During 1872, when the number diminished to one a week, he adopted the pen-name The Leisurely Saunterer.

The Zoroaster Higgins poems in *Hearth and Home:* "Ring Jingles," III, Aug. 26, 1871; "The Coroner's Verdict, Done into Rhyme by Zoroaster Higgins," III, Sept. 2, 1871; "The Suicide at Long Branch. Fluid Extract by Zoroaster Higgins," III, Sept. 9, 1871; " 'The Coming Race' As Seen by Zoroaster Higgins," III, Sept. 16, 1871; "The Muse of the American Institute," III, Sept. 23, 1871; "Who Stole the Vouchers? The Detective's Report. With Comments by Zoroaster Higgins," III, Sept. 30, 1871; "The Office-Seeker's Soliloquy," IV, June 22, 1872.

"Priscilla," *Scribner's Monthly,* III (Nov., 1871), 18-25. A short story, reprinted in *Duffels.*

"Mrs. Ardory, A Christmas Sketch in Three Chapters," *The Christian Union,* VI (Dec. 18, 1872), 504-5.

"The Christmas Club. A Ghost Story," *Scribner's Monthly*, V (Jan., 1873), 374-83. Reprinted in *Duffels*.

"Among the Elgin Watchmakers," *Scribner's Monthly*, V (March, 1873), following p. 656. Reprinted as a pamphlet, Chicago: Culver, Page, Hoyne and Co., Printers, n.d.

"Brother Moody," *The Christian Union*, IX (July 1, 1874), 511-12. About the evangelist, Dwight L. Moody.

"The Child-Garden," *The Christian Union*, X (July 15, 1874), 23. An article about the kindergarten.

"To the Saguenay Headlands," *The Christian Union*, X (Sept. 16, 1874), 204. Describing a trip with W. D. Howells.

"The Theatre Question," *The Christian Union*, X (Dec. 9, 1874), 454-55.

"The Prophet Novelist," *The Christian Union*, XI (March 3, 1875), 174-75. About George MacDonald.

"Professor Swing as a Preacher," *The Christian Union*, XI (May 12, 1875), 392-93. David Graham Swing was the radical clergyman, once tried for heresy, who installed Eggleston as pastor of the Church of Christian Endeavor.

"Denominational Peculiarities. Methodism," *The Christian Union*, XII (Sept. 22, 1875), 233.

"Dr. Holland the Moralist," *The Christian Union*, XII (Oct. 13, 1875), 297-98.

"Bobby and the Key-Hole," *St. Nicholas*, III (Jan., 1876), 184-90.

"The Child-Garden," *Scribner's Monthly*, XI (March, 1876), 615-28.

"Gypsying." *The Christian Union*, XIV (Sept. 6, 1876), 196.

"Bishop Janes," *The Christian Union*, XIV (Oct. 18, 1876), 308.

"The House of Santa Claus. A Christmas Fairy Show for Sunday-Schools," *St. Nicholas*, IV (Dec., 1876), 131-34.

"The Primitive Christian Church," *The Christian Union*, XIV (Dec. 20, 1876), 511-12.

"How P. P. Bliss Held the Fort," *The Christian Union*, XV (Jan. 17, 1877), 52-53.

Letters to the Brooklyn *Daily Times*, 1877: "Sights Abroad," July 10; "Trifles of Travel," July 31; "Glimpses of Paris," July 25.

"The New York Post Office," *Scribner's Monthly*, XVI (May, 1878), 59-79.

"Parsons and Parsons," *Scribner's Monthly*, XVII (Nov., 1878), 139-46.

"To the Clergy," *Scribner's Monthly*, XVII (March, 1879), 483-90. This and the preceding constitute an attack on cant, sanctimoniousness, pulpit mannerisms, and other clerical habits earning the contempt of thoughtful citizens.

"Some Recent Works of Fiction," *The North American Review*, CXXIX (Nov., 1879), 510-19.

*Selected Bibliography*

"Mother Goose and Her Family. A Christmas Recreation (For Sunday-school and Other Festivals)," *St. Nicholas*, VII (Dec., 1879), 146-49.

"Present Phases of Sunday-School Work," *Scribner's Monthly*, XIX (Feb., 1880), 524-31.

"George Eliot and the Novel," *The Critic*, I (Jan. 29, 1881), 9.

"Some Quacks," *Scribner's Monthly*, XXI (Feb., 1881), 620-24.

"Josiah Gilbert Holland," *The Century Magazine* (continuation of *Scribner's Monthly*), XXIII (Dec., 1881), 161-67.

"A Curious Drama," *St. Nicholas*, IX (Feb., 1882), 300-2.

"The Blessings of Piracy," *The Century Magazine*, XXIII (April, 1882), 942-45. An argument for international copyright.

"The Birthday Garden Party of Harriet Beecher Stowe," *The Atlantic Monthly*, L (Aug., 1882), a supplement of 16 pp.

Articles on American history in *The Century Magazine*: "The Beginning of a Nation," XXV (Nov., 1882), 61-83; "The Planting of New England," XXV (Jan., 1883), 350-66; "Migrations of American Colonists," XXV (March, 1883), 724-44; "The Aborigines and the Colonists," XXVI (May, 1883), 96-114; "Indian Wars in the Colonies," XXVI (Sept., 1883), 697-718; "Husbandry in Colonial Times," XXVII (Jan., 1884), 431-49; "Commerce in the Colonies," XXVIII (June, 1884), 234-56; "Social Conditions in the Colonies," XXVIII (Oct., 1884), 848-71; "The Colonists at Home," XXIX (April, 1885), 873-92; "Social Life in the Colonies," XXX (July, 1885), 387-407. "Church and Meeting House before the Revolution," XXXIII (April, 1887), 901-12; "The Church of England in the Colonies," XXXVI (May, 1888), 107-22; "Nathaniel Bacon, the Patriot of 1676," XL (July, 1890), 418-35.

"'Cash Down,' or a Percentage?" *The Critic*, IV (Feb. 9, 1884), 62. A contribution, dated Feb. 4, to a symposium of opinions by several authors.

"Americans at Play," *The Century Magazine*, XXVIII (Aug., 1884), 554-56. Reprinted in part in *The Phi Gamma Delta*, VII (Oct., 1884), 19-22.

"1809.—Oliver Wendell Holmes.—1884." *The Critic*, V (Aug. 30, 1884), 101. A symposium of tributes; Eggleston's letter runs to thirteen lines.

"Blaine vs. Cleveland. A Letter from Edward Eggleston." A letter dated Sept. 1, 1884, published as a pamphlet, one of a series issued by the National Committee of Republicans and Independents.

"A School of Long Ago," *St. Nicholas*, XII (July, 1885), 643-45.

"Sister Tabea," *The Century Magazine*, XXXI (April, 1886), 894-900. Reprinted in *Duffels*, and as a separate volume in 1896.

"A Lake George Capsize," *St. Nicholas*, XIII (Sept., 1886), 829-31.

"Books that Have Helped Me," *The Forum*, III (Aug., 1887), 578-86. One of a series by that title, written by various individuals, later collected in *Books that Have Helped Me* (New York, 1888). The first of Eggleston's reminiscences.

"The Federal Balance," *The Century Magazine*, XXXIV (Aug., 1887), 796-97.

"In Memoriam—Emma Lazarus," *The American Hebrew*, XXX (Dec. 9, 1887), 69.

"A Prospective Retrospect," *Harper's Weekly*, XXXI (Dec. 31, 1887), 958. A warning of conditions if the copyright bill should not pass.

"Anglo-American Copyright," *The North American Review*, CXLVI (Jan., 1888), 78-79. Contribution to a symposium of opinions.

"On the Writing of Novels," *The Critic*, XII (March 24, 1888), 135-38. A symposium; Eggleston's letter is on p. 136.

"Lincoln and 'The Graysons'," *The Critic*, XIII (Nov. 24, 1888), 260. A letter to the editor, dated Nov. 15, 1888.

"Tribute to James Russell Lowell," *The Critic*, XIV (Feb. 23, 1889), 92. A symposium contribution.

"A Full-Length History of the U. S.," *The Century Magazine*, XXXVII (March, 1889), 789-92.

"How a 'New' History Was Made," *The Critic*, XV (Aug. 17, 1889), 80. A letter to the editor, dated Aug. 2. Title supplied by the editor.

"The Advantages of a Country Boy," *The American Agriculturist*, XLIX (May, 1890), 274-75.

"Out-of-the-Ways in High Savoy," *The Century Magazine*, XL (Oct., 1890), 418-35.

"Formative Influences," *The Forum*, X (Nov., 1890), 279-90. One of a series with same title, by different authors.

"Ireland's Sad Fate," New York *World*, March 8, 1891.

"John White's Drawings," *The Nation*, LII (April 23, 1891), 340-41. A letter to the editor, dated April 9.

"Personal Tributes to Lowell," *The Writer*, V (Sept., 1891), 185-91. Eggleston's contribution is on pp. 187-88.

"Roswell Smith," *Harper's Weekly*, XXXVI (April 30, 1892), 416. An obituary tribute to a benefactor.

"Notes on the Completion of Mr. Parkman's Work," *The Century Magazine*, XLV (Nov., 1892), 46.

"The New Cashier," *The Century Magazine*, XLV (Dec., 1892), 189-91. A story, reprinted in *Duffels*.

"The Redemptioner. A Story in Three Scenes," *The Century Magazine*, XLVI (Dec., 1892), 625-34. Reprinted in *Duffels*.

*Selected Bibliography*

"The-Man-that-Draws-the-Handcart," *Harper's New Monthly Magazine*, LXXXVIII (Feb., 1894), 466-75. The magazine had accepted and paid for this article on George Northrup more than a quarter of a century before.

"Wild Flowers of English Speech in America," *The Century Magazine*, XLVII (April, 1894), 848-56. This and the next article reveal Eggleston as a pioneer in modern linguistic thinking.

"Folk-Speech in America," *The Century Magazine*, XLVIII (Oct., 1894), 867-75.

"Personal Tributes to Dr. Holmes," *The Writer*, VII (Nov., 1894), 161-83. Eggleston's letter is on p. 161.

"Advantages to Authors," New York *Times*, Dec. 9, 1894. Statement by Eggleston, p. 4. About the copyright law.

"Stevensoniana," *The Critic*, XXVI (Jan. 12, 1895), 29-33. Eggleston's contribution, "Mr. Eggleston's Words," p. 31.

"Authors on the Wheel," *The Critic*, XXVII (Oct. 12, 1895), 225-28. Eggleston's contribution to this symposium of opinions on the bicycle is on p. 227.

"Authors and Publishers on Arbitration," *The Critic*, XXX (Feb. 6, 1897), 87-90. One-sentence contribution, p. 87.

"Edward Eggleston: An Interview," *The Outlook*, LV (Feb. 6, 1897), 431-37. Mostly in Eggleston's own words.

"Honoring Mr. Stoddard," *The Critic*, XXX (April 3, 1897), 225-31. Eggleston's contribution is on p. 231.

"A Minnesota Storm," *Bubbles* (Madison, Indiana, High School), I (Dec., 1898), 1.

"The New History," *The American Historical Association Annual Report*, I (1900), 35-47. Reprinted in *Modern Eloquence*, ed. Thomas B. Reed (Philadelphia, 1900), Vol. VIII, pp. 401-12. Eggleston's presidential address.

"Letters of Congratulations on the Completion of *The Critic's* 20th Year," *The Critic*, XXXVIII (Jan. 15, 1901), 73-81. Eggleston's contribution is on p. 77.

## SECONDARY SOURCES

### I. *Books*

ÅHNEBRINK, LARS. *The Beginnings of Naturalism in American Fiction.* No. 9 of *Essays and Studies of American Language and Literature*, American Institute of the University of Upsala. Upsala and Cambridge, 1950. Especially pp. 50-59, 65. A European estimate of prime importance.

[An American Novelist and Preacher.] Pamphlet issued by Charles Scribner's Sons [1878]. No title page. An early critical estimate.

AURINGER, O[BADIAH] C[YRUS]. *Friendship's Crown of Verses; being*

*Memorials of Edward Eggleston.* Clinton, N. Y.: George Wm. Browning, 1907. A unique poetical tribute from a close friend.

BANTA, R. E. (compiler). *Indiana Authors and their Books.* Crawfordville: Wabash College, 1949. Pp. 96-98. A brief summary statement.

BLANCK, JACOB (compiler). *Bibliography of American Literature.* New Haven: Yale University Press, 1959. Vol. III. The most detailed listing of all editions of Eggleston's books.

BOWKER, R. R. *Copyright: Its History and Its Law.* Boston: Houghton Mifflin, 1912. Includes details of Eggleston's contribution to the copyright movement.

COAN, OTIS W. and RICHARD G. LILLARD. *America in Fiction: An Annotated List of Novels that Interpret Aspects of Life in the United States.* Stanford: Stanford University Press, 4th ed., 1956. Authoritative statements about Eggleston's novels.

COTTERILL, R. S. *The Old South.* Glendale: Arthur H. Clark Co., 1936. Background of the visit to Virginia.

COWIE, ALEXANDER. *The Rise of the American Novel.* New York: American Book Co., 1948. Includes a most sympathetic estimate of Eggleston's place in American fiction.

CURTISS, DANIEL S. *Western Portraiture, and Emigrants' Guide: a Description of Wisconsin, Illinois, and Iowa; with Remarks on Minnesota and Other Territories.* New York: J. H. Colton, 1852. Minnesota as Eggleston found it in 1856.

DONDORE, DOROTHY. *The Prairie and the Making of Middle America: 4 Centuries of Description.* Cedar Rapids: The Torch Press, 1926. A standard work on Midwestern writing.

E., F. G. [FRANCES GOODE EGGLESTON]. *Edward Eggleston. Authors Club Biography.* A pamphlet dated May, 1895.

EGGLESTON, GEORGE CARY. *The First of the Hoosiers, Reminiscences of Edward Eggleston.* . . . Philadelphia: Drexel Biddle, 1903. The first biography, an intimate memoir by a brother.

ESARY, LOGAN. *A History of Indiana,* Vol. II, *From 1850 to the Present.* Indianapolis: B. F. Bowen & Co., 1918. Background of Eggleston's native state.

GARLAND, HAMLIN. *A Daughter of the Middle Border.* New York: The Macmillan Co., 1917.

————. *Roadside Meetings.* New York: The Macmillan Co., 1930.

————. *My Friendly Contemporaries.* New York: The Macmillan Co., 1932. All three have personal reminiscences of Eggleston, and credit him with pioneering American realism.

GILDER, J. L. AND J. B. (eds.) *Authors at Home.* New York: A. Wessels Company, 1902. Includes an intimate sketch of Eggleston's home life.

GILDER, ROSAMOND (ed). *Letters of Richard Watson Gilder.* Boston:

Houghton Mifflin, 1916. Includes some Eggleston correspondence.

HOBART, CHAUNCEY. *History of Methodism in Minnesota.* Red Wing: Red Wing Printing Co., 1887. Includes information about Eggleston's work in Minnesota Methodism, written by a colleague.

HOWELLS, MILDRED. *Life in Letters of William Dean Howells.* New York: Doubleday, Doran, 1928. The relationship between Eggleston and Howells.

JOHNSON, ROBERT UNDERWOOD. *Remembered Yesterday.* Boston: Little, Brown, 1923. Facts about Eggleston's editorial positions and contributions to copyright.

KRAUS, MICHAEL. *A History of American History.* New York: Farrar and Rinehart, 1937. Includes an estimate of Eggleston as historian.

————. *The Writing of American History.* Norman: University of Oklahoma, 1953. A further estimate.

LOGAN, HARLAN DEBAUN. *An Unpublished Journal of Edward Eggleston's with Supplementary Letters.* Unpublished M. A. thesis, Indiana University, 1932. A major source of information, not elsewhere available, about the early years.

MCKINLEY, WILLIAM. *A Story of Minnesota Methodism.* Cincinnati: Jennings and Graham, 1911. Eggleston's progress as a preacher, recorded by a close friend.

*Minutes of the Minnesota Annual Conference of the Methodist Episcopal Church.* 1856-60, 1863-73. Factual information.

NEILL, E. D. *History of Ramsey County.* . . . Minneapolis: North Star Publishing Co., 1881. Background for the St. Paul period.

NICHOLSON, MEREDITH. *The Hoosiers.* New York: Macmillan, 1900. A careful, critical estimate.

————. *The Provincial American and Other Papers.* Boston: Houghton Mifflin, 1912.

OSBORNE, DUFFIELD. *The Authors Club: an Historical Sketch.* New York: Knickerbocker Press, 1913.

PAINE, STEPHEN. *A Critical Study of the Novels of Edward Eggleston.* Ann Arbor, Mich.: University Microfilms, 1962. Important critical analysis.

PARISH, EARNEST C. *A Brief History of the Church Known as Market Street, Jackson Street, Central Park.* St. Paul, 1933. Factual information about one of Eggleston's churches.

PHILLIPS, ULRICH B. *Life and Labor in the Old South.* Boston: Little, Brown, 1900. Standard book about the region.

QUINN, ARTHUR HOBSON (ed.). *Literature of the American People.* New York: Appleton, 1951. Especially Part 3, "The Later 19th Century," by Clarence Gohdes.

RANDEL, WILLIAM. *Edward Eggleston: Author of the Hoosier School-Master.* New York: King's Crown Press, 1946. More biographical than critical.

SCUDDER, SAMUEL (using pen-name A. Rochester Fellow): *The Winnipeg Country, or Roughing It with an Eclipse Party.* Boston: Cupples, Upham, & Co., 1886. Corroborates Eggleston's newspaper reports of the 1860 eclipse expedition.

*Statistical Gazeteer of the State of Virginia . . . to 1854.* Richmond: printed for Richard Edwards, 1855. Background.

STEDMAN, LAURA, and GEORGE GOULD. *Life and Letters of Edmund Clarence Stedman.* New York: Moffat, Yard & Co., 1910. Literary memorabilia.

TAYLOR, WALTER F. *The Story of American Letters.* Chicago: Henry Regnery, 1956. General critical evaluation.

TOOKER, LEWIS FRANK. *The Joys and Tribulations of an Editor.* New York: The Century Co., 1924. Includes valuable facts about Eggleston as an editor.

VAN DOREN, CARL. *The American Novel: 1789-1939.* New York: Macmillan, 1940. General literary evaluation, sympathetic to Eggleston.

VEDDER, H. C. *American Writers of Today.* New York: Silver, Burdett, 1894. An evaluation of Eggleston during his lifetime.

VENABLE, W. H. *The Beginnings of Literary Culture in the Ohio Valley.* Cincinnati: Robert Clarke & Co., 1891. Good for literary background of Eggleston's writing.

II. *Articles (in chronological order)*

"The P. G. D. Convention," Indianapolis *Evening News,* May 3, 1872. A report of Eggleston's address to the Phi Gamma Delta convention.

BOYESEN, HJALMAR. "The Realism of the American Fiction," *The Independent,* XLIV (Nov. 3, 1872), 1543-44. An early estimate of Eggleston's place among realistic authors.

[Note on Eggleston], *The Christian Union,* VII (May 14, 1873, 381.

GLADDEN, WASHINGTON. "Edward Eggleston," *Scribner's Monthly,* VI (September, 1873), 561-64. A rather eulogistic estimate by a man somewhat in Eggleston's debt.

"Edward Eggleston, D. D.," *The Phrenological Journal,* LXI (Dec., 1875), 376-79. A pseudo-scientific character analysis.

"Novel Church Enterprise," New York *Tribune,* Dec. 27, 1877. About the Church of Christian Endeavor.

"Writers Who Lack College Training," *The Critic,* IX (Dec. 11, 1886), 296-97.

Selected Bibliography

"The Author of *Roxy*," *The Book Buyer*, IV (April, 1887), 96-97.
AURINGER, O. C. "Dr. Edward Eggleston at Lake George," *The Critic*, XI (Sept. 3, 1887), 111-12.
"An Authors Club," *The Critic*, XIII (Dec. 2, 1888), 328-29. An early description of the purpose and activities of the Authors' Club.
ZIMMERMAN, JANE EGGLESTON. "Edward Eggleston," *The Epworth Herald*, April 22, 1893. A sister's estimate.
MARTIN, EARLE E. "In His Hoosier Home," Chicago *Tribune*, July 30, 1893. A description of Eggleston's temporary quarters in Madison, Indiana.
"A Reception to Dr. Eggleston," *The Critic*, XXIX (Dec. 12, 1896), 389-90. A report of the Authors' Club tribute after publication of *The Beginners of a Nation*.
"Edward Eggleston's Two Eras," *Munsey's Magazine*, XVI (March, 1897), 755-56. Eggleston as novelist and historian.
JOHNSON, ROSSITER. "The Author's Club," *The Critic*, XXX (May 8, 1897), 315-17.
ZIMMERMAN, C. H. "Edward Eggleston: Methodist Preacher, Novelist Historian," *The Epworth Herald*, March 25, 1899. A brother-in-law's opinion.
EGGLESTON, GEORGE CARY. "Edward Eggleston: His Home, His Manner of Living, His Surroundings, Habits, Tastes, and Way of Work," New York *Times Literary Review*, Nov. 9, 1901.
BRAGDON, CHARLES C. "Edward Eggleston at Home," *Zion's Herald*, Sept. 10, 1902. The last interview before Eggleston died.
"Edward Eggleston," *The Outlook*, LXXII (Sept. 13, 1902), 102. An obituary comment.
AURINGER, O. C. "Edward Eggleston: A Memorial Sonnet," *The Critic*, XLI (Oct., 1902), 332.
CARY, EDWARD. "Dr. Edward Eggleston," *The Book Buyer*, XXV (Oct., 1902), 221-23.
NICHOLSON, MEREDITH. "Edward Eggleston," *The Atlantic Monthly*, XC (Dec., 1902), 804-9.
EGGLESTON, GEORGE CARY. "First of the Hoosiers," *The Outlook*, LXXVIII (Oct. 8, 1904), 382-83. Later expanded into the book of the same title.
WARD, WILLIAM HAYES. "Sixty Years of the Independent," *The Independent*, LXV (Dec. 10, 1908), 1345-51.
JAMESON, J. F. "The American Historical Association, 1884-1909," *The American Historical Review*, XV (Oct., 1909), 11. Includes facts about Eggleston's participation and presidency.
KNOX, J. L. "Vevay and Switzerland County," *Indiana Magazine of History*, XI (Sept., 1915), 216-30. Good for background.

DANGLADE, ANETTE. "Early Days in Switzerland County," *Indiana Magazine of History*, XIII (June, 1917), 151-56. Early days of Vevay.

GARBER, BLANCHE GOODE. "Judge Miles Carey Eggleston," *Indiana Magazine of History*, XVII (Sept., 1921), 243-56. Factual.

"An Interpreter of Early Indiana History," *The Christian Science Monitor,* Aug. 25, 1923. A fair critical estimate.

TOOKER, L. FRANK. "As I Saw from an Editor's Desk," *The Century Magazine*, CVIII (June, 1924), 268-71. About Eggleston as a contributor.

JOHNSON, MERLE. "American First Editions. Edward Eggleston (1837-1902)," *The Publishers' Weekly*, CXIX (May 16, 1931), 2245-46. Bibliographical data.

RUSK, RALPH LESLIE. "Edward Eggleston," *Dictionary of American Biography*, V (New York: Charles Scribner's Sons, 1931), 52-54. A reliable brief biographic sketch.

RABB, KATE MILNER. "The Hoosier Listening Post," Indianapolis *Star*, June 17, 1931. With a letter from Archibald Shaw, who as a boy witnessed Eggleston's return from Virginia.

BLOOM, MARGARET. "Eggleston's Notes on Hoosier Dialect," *American Speech*, IX (Dec., 1934), 319-20.

DANNER, EFFA MORRISON. "Edward Eggleston," *Indiana Magazine of History*, XXXIII (Dec., 1937), 435-53. A centennial article of prime biographical importance.

FLANAGAN, JOHN T. "The Hoosier Schoolmaster in Minnesota," *Minnesota History*, XVIII (Dec., 1937), 347-70. Another centennial article of importance, representing the pioneer research into the Minnesota period.

ACKERMAN, GERTRUDE. "George Northrup, Frontier Scout," *Minnesota History*, XIX (Dec., 1938), 377-92.

STONE, EDWARD. "Edward Eggleston's Religious Transit," *University of Texas Studies in English*, No. 3926 (July, 1939), 210-18. The evolution of Eggleston's religious thinking.

RAWLEY, JAMES A. "Some New Light on Edward Eggleston," *American Literature*, XI (Jan., 1940), 453-58. Previously unrecorded biographic insights.

HIRSCHFELD, CHARLES. "Edward Eggleston: Pioneer in Social History," *Historiography and Urbanization: Essays in Honor of W. Stull Holt,* ed. Eric F. Goldman (Baltimore: the Johns Hopkins Press, 1941), pp. 189-210. A careful estimate of Eggleston's place among historians.

FLANAGAN, JOHN T. "The Novels of Edward Eggleston," *College English*, V (Feb., 1944), 250-54. A good critical review of the major fiction.

RAWLEY, JAMES A. "Edward Eggleston: Historian," *Indiana Magazine of History*, XL (Dec., 1944), 341-52. A critical evaluation.

HALLER, JOHN M. "Edward Eggleston, Linguist," *Philological Quarterly*, XXIV (April, 1945), 175-86. Eggleston considered as an amateur linguistic scholar.

RANDEL, WILLIAM. "Edward Eggleston's Library at Traverse des Sioux," *Minnesota History*, XXVI (Sept., 1945), 242-47. The specific books owned at the age of twenty-one.

————. "Zoroaster Higgins: Edward Eggleston as a Political Satirist in Verse," *American Literature*, XVII (Nov., 1945), 255-60.

JOHANNSEN, ROBERT. "Literature and History: the Early Novels of Edward Eggleston," *Indiana Magazine of History*, XLVIII (March, 1952), 37-54.

RANDEL, WILLIAM. "Edward Eggleston's Minnesota Fiction," *Minnesota History*, XXXIII (Spring, 1953), 189-93.

———— (ed., with intro.). "The Kit Carson of the Northwest," *Minnesota History*, XXXIII (Autumn, 1953), 269-81. A reprinting of the article on George Northrup.

———— "Edward Eggleston on Dialect," *American Speech*, XXX (May, 1955), 111-14. Eggleston's criticism of a college professor's article on Negro speech.

ESARY, LOGAN. "Elements of Culture in the Old Northwest," *Indiana Magazine of History*, LIII (1957), 257-64. General cultural background.

TAYLOR, ARCHER. "Proverbial Materials in Edward Eggleston, *The Hoosier Schoolmaster*," *Studies in Folklore*, ed. W. Edson Richmond (Bloomington: University of Indiana Press, 1957), pp. 262-70. A scholarly analysis of Eggleston's use of folk sayings.

# Index